Y0-BSL-738

GLENDALE PUBLIC LIBRARY, CA

3 9010 02151 4611

GLENDALE PUBLIC LIBRARY
GLENDALE, CALIFORNIA
REFERENCE

Collings, Adam
Randolph (Randy)
Yosemite and the
High Sierra

R
917.9447
COW

Special Collections Room
Not to be taken from the Library
U-53A

YOSEMITE

— AND —

THE HIGH SIERRA

YOSEMITE
— AND —
THE HIGH SIERRA

Written, Designed and Edited
by
Randy Collings

R
917.9447
COL

YOSEMITE
— AND —
THE HIGH SIERRA

Featuring the Photography of
Ed Cooper
and
William Neill
with
James Blank, Emil Forler
Mark Gibson and Roy Murphy

Published in the United States
by

ADAM RANDOLPH COLLINGS
i n c o r p o r a t e d

BOX 8658 • HOLIDAY STATION
ANAHEIM, CALIFORNIA 92802

This book was printed by Jefferies Lithograph, Carson, California, from LithoFilm prepared by Jefferies Lithograph. Typography
and mechanicals by American Graphic & Stationers, Anaheim, California.

COVER: Majestic Half Dome rises above the waters of the Merced River in California's famed Yosemite Valley.
FRONT GATE: The sheer whitewater curtain of Yosemite's Vernal Falls. Photograph by James Blank.
TITLE PAGE: Dogwood blossoms signal springtime in the high Sierra. Photograph by William Neill.
FRONTISPIECES IN ORDER: Majestic Sentinel and the South Wall of Yosemite Valley. Photograph by William Neill – Fall colors in the high Sierra. Photograph by William Neill. – Summer scene of woods and meadows in Yosemite Valley. Photograph by William Neill. – Storm clouds and waterfalls spill over the rim of Yosemite Valley. Photograph by William Neill.
THIS PAGE: Half Dome catches the fading light of day at sunset. Photograph by Mark Miller.
LAST PAGE: Stark splendor at Iceberg Lake. Photograph by Ed Cooper.
BACK COVER: American Black Bear. Photograph by Stephen J. Krasemann.

Library of Congress Catalog Card Number: 85-090900

THE·AMERICAN·EXPERIENCE

©1985 by Adam Randolph Collings, Inc.

introduction

DAVID GRABER

With topographic features and geologic design so extraordinary and rare, a written description of the grand Sierra Nevada, that great timbered wall shielding California's bounty from the stark desolation of a desert wasteland, proves elusive if not impossible. Superlatives, rhetoric, and adjectives exhausted, the author still finds the stupendous scene before him inadequately portrayed for the reader on paper. Tapered peaks, raging cataracts, prehistoric sequoia giants and massive mountains must be seen and experienced first hand if they are to be properly comprehended and fully appreciated.

Couple such natural grandeur with the pageantry of human history in the Far West and you find yourself confronted with a challenge fit for Cecil B. DeMile.

It is the author's hope that readers will vicariously thrill to a land and history that has intrigued him since childhood when his father first introduced him to its high country splendor. To the reader he extends celebrated John Muir's invitation:

"Climb the mountains and get their good tidings. Nature's peace will flow into you as sunshine flows into trees. The winds will blow their own freshness into you, and the storms their energies, while cares will drop off like autumn leaves."

ROBERT GROVE

BRET R. LUNDBERG

PROLOGUE

Traveling west, across the North American continent, one marvels as undulating hills and forested mountains of emerald green give way to the endless steppes and grasslands of the Great Plains. Soon, along the horizon, breathtaking stone battlements appear as you approach the famed Rocky Mountains. Pine-clad slopes and snow-covered peaks are shrouded in a rich Western heritage of pioneer folklore. Upon clearing the Wasatch Front, alongside Salt Lake, you leave behind the last vestiges of the Rockies to traverse stark desolation in the Great Basin.

Surprisingly enough the splendor and charm left behind remains yet to be surpassed; for that which lies ahead supersedes all of America's magnificence, be it real or imagined.

Suddenly you see the great wall that protects it, rising above sagebrush and saline sinks in unrivaled grandeur; a gigantic escarpment whose saw-toothed ridge surmounts 14,000 feet in height; holding at bay the endless desolation spread out before it.

Timbered walls, not unlike those of fictional Midian, shield from view a spectacular land of unsurpassed beauty and abundance. Bastions of granite conceal a treasure so enchanting and rare that once discovered men have risked their very lives to attain it.

Unlike the Rockies, these great mountains afford no passage, no lowlands between peaks, no break in the chain. To reach fabled El Dorado, one must scale its vertical palisades or trek through hundreds of miles of torrid desert sands to bypass its barrier. The longest, highest, and, by most accounts, grandest range of mountains in North America, it effectively impeded invasion, harboring a realm so unique and detached from the rest of the world as to seem the product of fancy rather than reality.

It is to this great wall, "The Range of Light," more commonly known as the Sierra Nevada, that we herein focus our attentions, and to the unparalleled splendor of its glacier-sculptured heart – the Yosemite.

The Last Trail

I

Across the bison-dotted plain
  Where plodding thousands pressed,
He wandered with a wagon train
  To seek the fabled West.

Not twenty yet!—but lithe and stout
  As a gale-resisting pine,
He had heard the golden bugles shout
  In the airs of 'Forty Nine;

And forth from his green Virginia home,
  He had burst like a colt set free,
Called by the wind and sky to roam,
  And beckoned by peak and tree.

But as he lumbered along the trail
  Over the rutted grass,
His goal seemed less than a dreamer's tale
  Beside one twinkling lass,—

Ellen, the daughter of their guide,
  A maiden rosy-fair;
Supple of limb, and amber-eyed,
  And dowered with auburn hair,
Whose gaze had a flash of stinging pride
  That was the lad's despair!

II

Long in his memory, like a scourge,
  He heard her scorn recur,
When, faltering-tongued, he tried to urge
  A rendezvous with her.

"O Danny Long!" her laughter trilled,
  But shook him like a blast.
"Your wish perhaps shall be fulfilled
  When you're a man at last!

And, laughing still, she tripped away;
  But ever he bore the scar.
And ever vowing, "I'll have my day!"
  He worshipped from afar.

Among the weedy flats they rolled,
  And toiled up long inclines
Where mountains loomed remote and cold,
  Like white, Titantic shrines.

And over the winding timber land,
  Peopled by wolf and bear. . .
Till they saw the salt plateaux expand
  With a far, eye-wounding glare.

Then on, across a starving vast
  Where the thirsty oxen fell,
And the mountains, strewn with sagebrush, cast
  A spirit-clouding spell.

Even their leader's granite brow
  Was furrowed with grim alarm:
"Make haste! We're late already now!"
  He shouted, with upraised arm.

"Make haste! The winter comes! It comes,
  And frosty mounds pile high!
Hear how the winds, like threatening drums,
  Roar from the chilling sky!

But slower and slower lagged the horde,
  And the weak began to quail.
And half a score could trudge no more
  Along the weary trail.

And half a score in silence lay,
  With crosses to mark their rest,
Far on the huge and lonely gray
  Of the desert's broken breast.

III

Scarce forty rovers, tattered and torn
  And gaunt with the rationed fare,
Arrived, when autumn was newly born,
  Where the carved Sierras stare,—

The bleak Sierras, snowy-browed
  And ragged with fir and pine,
Beyond whose spires, the guide avowed,
Were valleys free of snow or cloud
  And flowing in milk and wine!

But oh, the miles and miles between!—
  The twisted hundred miles
Along the rim of the gnarled ravine
  And the shadowy forest aisles!

Had but the mountains raised a rod
  And bidden the wind to rest,
The tired wanderers would have trod
  The warm and honeyed West;

But surely some maniac hand controlled
  The leashes of the gale.
Too early came the winter cold,
  And whitened the pilgrim trail.

Too early came the winter cold,
  With snow-drifts shoulder-tall,
And solid ranks of icy banks,
  Like some beleaguering wall!. . .

How wracked the faces Danny Long
  Viewed in the shivering camp,—
Trail-hardened men, once iron-strong,
  Now with a skeleton stamp!—

And whimpering women, thin and white
  As ghosts that came and passed,
Where the blazing logs threw back the night
  But not the chattering blast.

"If only the storm will end, will end,
  We'll push to the sunlit vale!"
But the sleet continued to descend,
  Lashed by a scourging gale.

And the sleet continued to descend,
  And famine was prowling nigh.
And the lean, sick oxen had to lend
  The only food supply.

"When these are gone? When these are gone?
  The feverish plaint arose.
But the men, their brooding eyes withdrawn,
  Stared at the gathering snows.

"Rations for barely three weeks more!
  Three hungry weeks!" they said.
And the wind let out a screech and a roar
  Like mockery of their dread.

"There is one hope!" the whispered word
  Went flashing round the camp.
And the forlorn, desperate scheme they heard
  Burned like a smoldering lamp.

"Should any man, as a last resort,
  Plunge to the plain below,
He'll find a place—called Sutter's Fort—
  Whence help for all may flow!"

Now on the men a silence fell,
  And they nodded with mirthless smiles.
Who would set out on that frozen route
  For a hundred trackless miles?

Better to die where warm lights glow,
  With their women and their kin,
Than to fall alone in the night and snow
  Where engulfing blizzards spin!

IV

As Danny Long, with sunken eyes,
  Gazed on the blue-lipped crowd,
A startled hope began to rise
  From his spirit's wrack and cloud.

Beside an icy-hooded man
  He peered at the wasted face
Of her who, when their course began,
  Had laughed with lily grace.

And a message in her desolate glance,
  Her ghostly-fragile cheeks,
Lashed out, and smote him like a lance:
  "We die, and no man speaks!"

"Hear me! I speak!" cried Danny Long.
  "I go! I take the trail!"
And the weary eyes of the wondering throng
  Answered, "To what avail?"

But careless of all his comrades said,
  He hastened the reckless flight.
For in the eyes of a maid he read
  A sudden grateful light.

V

The clearing sky was palely blue
  And the hooting wind had died,
When Danny waved a brisk adieu
  And mounted a white divide;
While three companions—a haggard crew—
  Stalked grayly at his side.

Over a bouldery ridge, and down
  An iced precipitous aisle,
And through ravines with a piny crown,
  They wandered in single file.

For hours, amid the mounded snow
  That piled about their knees,
Their weakening footsteps pressed below
  Through winding leagues of trees.

For hours they followed a river track,
  And recognized the way
By tatters of clothes, and heaps of black
  Where abandoned wagons lay.

And horns of cattle lined their path;
  And sleek wolves nosed in sight.
And here and there, with grisly glare,
  A skull of glittering white.

By evening the chargers of the gale
  Tore through a shrieking land.
And the damp-log fires, smoky and pale,
  Blinked on a cowering band;

While in the morning's pelted gloom
  They crept to the trail again
Like shadows stealing from a tomb,—
  Shadows that once were men.

Like shadows stealing from a tomb
  After some ghoulish rite,
Mutely they dared the tempest-doom
  And the billowing sweeps of white.

But long before that howling day
  Had snorted to a close,
One of the starved adventurers lay
  Silent amid the snows.

Shallow the grave they dug for him
  There in the screeching cold.
But the living three heard distantly
  Their own bleak dirges tolled.

Then forth once more into the blast
  Where the creaking pine-trees strained . . .
Till, when another dawn was past,
  But two of the men remained.

Now Danny, as he dragged his way
  Across the sneering wild
Beheld his sole companion sway
  And whimper like a child . . .

Then fall to earth . . . and the rainy sky
  Sobbed like a lost soul's moan.
And the youth knelt down; and, with a sigh,
  Followed the trail alone.

VI

Far through the canyon's dim descent
  He made his faltering way,
To slopes where dwarfish oaks were bent
  Under a roof of gray.

And down and down, unceasingly,
  Gnawing at roots for food,
Where, through wide hill-lands, he could see
  No end to the solitude.

Only the thought of an ice-bound camp
  In a spectral, bluish waste,
Upheld his steps on the tortured tramp
  And murmured and cried, "Make haste!"

Only the memory of a maid
  Pleading with ravaged eyes,
Stabbed at his heart as he kneeled, and prayed
  To the showery, heedless skies.

"O Danny Long!" her laughter trilled
  Out of the mocking past.
"Your wish for me shall be fulfilled
  When you're a man at last!"

"Oh, may my wish be soon fulfilled!"
  He muttered, half aloud.
But "Never!" the jeering north wind shrilled
  From her rags of scudding cloud.

Now, with delirium in his brain
  And a trembling in his limbs,
He sees the stretch of the great brown plain,
  A plain that whirls and swims . . .

And he droops and sinks, to rise once more
  And stumble along the trail,

Devoured by fires that shrivel and roar,
  And demons that howl, "You fail!"
But he staggers still by pond and hill,
  Moaning, "I must prevail!"

VII

Sprawled in the mire beneath an oak
  In the mirthful valley sun,
Two Indians saw the mud-stained cloak
  Of him who was spent and done.

And they carefully gathered up the lad,
  Hoping he yet might live,
But saw that he gasped for speech, and had
  A message of blood to give.

"High up the trail—they waste away—
  Help them—the time is short!"
Such was the prayer they heard him pray
  When hastened to Sutter's Fort.

But as he tossed on a new-made bed,
  Huddled in warm, dry clothes,
He knew that a rescuing party sped
  Over the hills and snows;

And again he saw a maiden's face
  And the sparkling glance she cast;
And she smiled with a golden, rose-hued grace:
  "O Danny Long, you've won the race
  And earned your wish at last!"

And the weary lids drew closed once more,
  And quiet slumber came;
And the final word his faint lips bore
  Was the echo of her name.

The final word his faint lips bore
  Was, "Tell her I shall wait
Where never numbing snow can pour
  Nor storm-gale scream its hate."

Then, with that smile of bright content
  Known to the blessed few,
He slipped away like one who went
  To a lover's rendezvous ♥

STANTON A. COBLENTZ

YOSEMITE

— AND ———

THE HIGH SIERRA

MOUNT WHITNEY

TULE ELK

Defined as being limited on the north by the Feather River Canyon south of volcanic Lassen Peak and on the south by Tehachapi Pass above Los Angeles, the Sierra Nevada stretches nearly five hundred miles along the eastern boundary of California. A magnificent unit, heralded as one of the finest examples on the face of the globe of a single, contiguous range, it varies in breadth from forty to eighty miles. So asymmetrical in design is it, however, that its crest consistently lies within a few miles of its eastern base, with one notable exception near Lake Tahoe where a secondary escarpment juts out across the western boundary of the Carson Valley.

Dr. Francois E. Matthes, noted geologist and lifelong friend of the Yosemite, fancied Mary Austin's likening of the great Sierra Range to a gigantic ocean wave rolling landward from the west. "Rising in a grand sweep from the trough of the great Valley (California's extensive Central Valley)," he once wrote, "this giant wave culminates in a somewhat sinuous snowy top, as in a foam crest, and with its precipitous front, threatens the low lying deserts to the east."

There could scarcely be a more complete antithesis between geographic features of the earth's surface than that which exists between the mighty "Range of Light" and the extensive lowlands that adjoin it on either side.

To the west lies the great Central Valley, a featureless plain burnished gold under perennial California sunshine. Well watered by Sierra snowshed, it has become the most prolific agricultural empire in the world. Here, a year round growing season provides for billion dollar harvests, supplying much of America and the world with its bounty.

To the east of the high Sierra stretches the Great Basin. In stark contrast to the Central Valley this vast barren province of sagebrush plain is itself interspersed with titled block ranges, each duplicating the grand Sierra on a diminutive scale. California's great Central Valley lies at a mere 100 feet above sea level. The lowlands of the Great Basin sit at an elevation somewhere between 3,000 and 6,000 feet. Rivers emanating from the mountain massif and watering the Central Valley include the Feather, Yuba, American, Mokolumne, Stanislaus, Tuolumne, Merced, San Joaquin, Kings and Kaweah. All but the last of these continue flowing westward into San Francisco Bay. Sierra born watershed flowing eastward in river systems such as the Truckee, Carson, Walker, and Owens evaporate amidst the parched desert sands of "playas" or dry lakes. Several outstanding exceptions to this rule are the briny "seas" at Great Salt Lake, west of the Wasatch, Mono Lake, east of Yosemite and Owens Lake, southeast of Mt. Whitney.

Standing on the crest of the high Sierra one is struck with the awesome contrasts just described. To the west stretches one of the earth's most spectacular timber belts; a well watered, forest-clad range, that disappears amidst the Central Valley's golden glow and the azure hue of the Pacific. Eastward, as far as the eye can see, unfurls a desolate land of little rain.

24

The Sierra Nevada itself is largely responsible for this interesting paradox. A "climatic maker," it is to a large extent the author of its own weather conditions. Running parallel to the ocean, this great upland forms an awesome barrier over which moisture-laden winds from the Pacific must rise. Thus, forced ever higher, zephyrs chill and discharge their condensed water vapor, showering the range with an abundance of precipitation. Most of this moisture is harvested during the winter season in the form of snow; Sierra summers being remarkably dry. As one might suspect, given the name of the range (Sierra Nevada meaning snowy mountains), snow is one of the Sierra's most striking features. Its abundance in winter exceeds that of any other region in the lower "forty-eight" states (with the single exception of occasional competition for pre-eminence by that of the Cascade mountains in the extreme northwest), thus giving the range its general snow-clad appearance.

Annual snowfall between altitudes of 6,000 and 7,000 feet averages 10 to 20 feet. During some winters it will surpass 30 feet. By the time Pacific air streams surmount the dizzying heights of the high Sierra they have been wrung dry, hence the barren nature of the land to the leeward side.

Though occasional thunderstorms occur throughout the summer months, precipitation from June through August is nominal, affording a delightful high country Shangri La. Such salubrious and enjoyable conditions have enticed man, since the days of the American Indian, to seek out the highlands, gathering there to escape the searing heat of summer in the lowlands.

Traversing "The Wall," albeit next to impossible during winter months, affords a delightful adventure to the naturalist and outdoor enthusiast during the spring and summer.

Due to its geographic position and topographic features, the Sierra Nevada contains a remarkable variety of climactic conditions and biological expressions. Indeed, a mere crossing of the range from west to east might be compared with an entire voyage through the numerous life zones encountered on a journey extending from northern Mexico to the American Arctic.

Ascending from its western foothills one travels through a vast sloping grassland. Here and there magnificent oak trees spread their outstretched branches, offering shade in an otherwise hot, dry environ. During California's wet, rainy season, when blizzards close Sierra mountain passes, the lush verdure of these hills remains unrivalled by even the most tropical of settings. Later, as the high country adorns itself in summer greenery, these lowlands, their raucus explosion of wild flowers and finery having spent itself, assume the golden tint of autumn. This vestment they will wear throughout the remainder of the year.

Just above these grassy steppes, rising at a gentle gradient of only 2 to 6 percent, begins an impenetrable chaparral belt. Slopes become densely clad with small-leaved live-oak, buckbrush, chinquapin and manzanita.

Beyond stretch the magnificent forests of the middle slope. Pine, fir, and incense cedar here attain heights of up to 250 feet. A

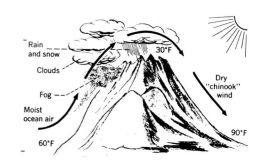

AS MOIST OCEAN AIR RISES UP THE WINDWARD SLOPES OF THE SIERRA NEVADA IT COOLS, WATER VAPOR CONDENSES, AND CLOUDS FORM. AS THE AIR CONTINUES TO RISE AND COOL, RAIN OR SNOW FALLS ON THE HIGHER SLOPES. BY THE TIME THE AIR REACHES THE MOUNTAINTOPS AND BEGINS TO FLOW DOWN THE LEEWARD SLOPES, IT HAS LOST MUCH OF ITS MOISTURE. THUS THE LEEWARD SLOPES OF THE MOUNTAINS RECEIVE LESS RAINFALL THAN THE WINDWARD SLOPES, AND THE DRY LANDS TO THE EAST ARE SAID TO BE IN THE "RAIN SHADOW" OF THE MOUNTAINS.

CALIFORNIA VALLEY OAK

25

GIANT SEQUOIA
(Sequoiandendron giganteum)

zone of superlative tree growth, this is also the realm of the giant sequoia, largest living thing on earth. In isolated groves these redwood monarchs, thousands of years old, raise their hoary heads above the forest canopy, commanding both awe and respect for their sheer massiveness and primitive grace.

Still farther up, into the lodgepole pine belt, where the snowdrifts linger into mid-summer, tree stature begins to diminish. At timber line only recumbent dwarf dendroids brave a region of harsh sub-arctic conditions. Although brief, summer here is extremely pleasurable. Rock bound sapphire lakes, babbling brooks swollen with snow melt, and viridescent high country meadows colored with a myriad of wildflowers glisten in the thin atmosphere beneath a resplendent blue sky.

Near the crest of the range, stark summit peaks shelter deeply sculpted natural amphitheaters. Herein remnant glaciers, composed of the accumulated snows from a thousand years, glisten. Precipitation, even during summer months, descends in the form of hail and snow flurries. These extensive highlands stretch between towering crags and glacial cirques, inviting the more adventurous to explore their eerie isolated grandeur.

Beyond such snow flecked peaks, the great Sierra escarpment drops off suddenly. A two-mile high wall rises abruptly from the sands and sage of the Great Basin. Along this eastern front the life zones previously described are repeated. Yet, whereas each transition occurred across expanses miles wide on the western slopes, here transformations are evident every several thousand feet as you descend the near-vertical bulwark.

On this journey, from west to east, across the great range, one traverses the famed Mother Lode. Here California's Gold Rush transformed a sleepy Spanish province into a progressive Yankee empire. Remnants of mining camps and boomtowns still riddle the western foothills, while the eastern slope holds the last vestments of the great silver boom, with its world-renowned Comstock Lode and gaudy Virginia City.

A virtual fantasia of geology and geography is encountered – incomparable hidden valleys chiseled by glaciers, mile-high waterfalls and raging cataracts racing over granite cliffs, through canyons and gorges thousands of feet deep, giant domes of once molten granite – a wilderness wonderland.

Deep within forested glades great bears and panthers still roam the woods. Secluded mountain meadows are graced by elegant deer. Stark precipices, animated by rare Sierra Bighorn and tiny rock pikas, pierce the skyline. Pristine beauty in the high country and the spectacular crystal clear waters of Lake Tahoe are experienced.

Lastly one beholds the great wall itself, rising above Owens Valley, where rare Tule elk roam in the shadows of 14,495 foot Mt. Whitney, highest point in the continental United States.

By what means has such grandeur come to be? As man's knowledge increases, his understanding of the powers of creation is expanded and altered, sometimes making it necessary to transcend previously cherished theories. One can only speculate as to the true origins of the mighty Sierra Nevada. Nevertheless, a viable explanation does seem to exist.

eeply carved into the western flank of the Range of Light, about midway between torrid foothills and wintry summits, literally and figuratively at the very heart of California, lies Yosemite Valley.

Of all the approaches to this earthly paradise perhaps that along Wawona Road affords its most dramatic port of entry. Emerging from a mile-long tunnel, in one breath-taking, sweeping view, the entire Yosemite panorama is disclosed. Once having entered the valley, from whatever route, one is no longer left in doubt as to the reason for its world-renowned acclaim.

"The Incomparable Valley," it has been known to bring tears to the eyes of those gazing out at its unsurpassed beauty. from Inspiration Point. No other valley seems so remarkably fashioned. No other valley holds within so small an area such an astounding array of distinctive features.

A broad, glacial-hewn trough, some seven miles long and one-half to one mile across, it forms a wide floor in the middle of the Merced River Canyon. Parallel sides stand out boldly sculptured and adorned with some of the world's highest waterfalls. Like an enormous unroofed cathedral, at its apse stands the soaring granite altar known as Half Dome. Here to worship, some 2.6 million annual visitors make the pilgrimage to what has clearly emerged as the "Mona Lisa" of the wilderness.

The Valley of Yosemite is but a small, albeit integral, part of the Sierra preserve known as Yosemite National Park. Stretching across 760,917 acres (an area roughly the size of the state of Rhode Island), the Park itself contains a seemingly endless variety of wonders and natural treasures.

Less than a dozen miles to the north of the famed valley, and running almost parallel to it, is the Grand Canyon of the Tuolumne River. This profound gash exceeds the Yosemite in both length and depth, though scarcely in scenic grandeur. It terminates in the beautiful Hetch Hetchy Valley, a lesser Yosemite, that has since been impounded by a dam (further south, beyond the Yosemite, Kings Canyon is framed by stupendous walls rising 7,000 to 8,000 feet from streambed to summit).

Yosemite Valley's Merced River flows tumultuously into its high mountain chamber where, its pace diminished, the raging torrent is transformed into a meandering watercourse. Once beyond the valley floor, it rages again, cascading through rugged terrain to the broad expanse of the Central Valley below.

Both the canyons of the Tuolumne and the Merced Rivers form two long furrows in the western flank of the Sierra Nevada – two of a great series of such furrows, all of notable depth and nearly all arranged roughly parallel to one another, running at right angles to the crestline of the range. The Yosemite, therefore, is but one chasm in a land of many chasms.

On either side of Yosemite's vast mountain declivity, great cliffs reach skyward to forested uplands. These timbered plateaus extend, unbroken by side canyons, to the head of the famed Valley. There a convergence of three great depressions

YOSEMITE (ANGELICIZED FROM THE INDIAN WORD UHUMATI) MEANS GRIZZLY BEAR. HENCE YOSEMITE IS THE VALLEY OF THE GRIZZLY BEAR. TO THE SIERRA MIWOK WHO INHABITED THE VALLEY, HOWEVER, IT WAS KNOWN AS AHWAHNEE OR VALLEY OF THE TALL GRASS.

(continued on page 30)

27

THE GIANT SEQUOIA

The oldest giant sequoias now standing in the forests of the Sierra Nevada sprouted back when mankind had barely learned the meaning of civilization. As the pageantry of human history unfolded each Sierra redwood progressed through its life cycle, growing taller and stronger, producing seed by the millions to perpetuate its noble race, spreading roots outward from its mammoth base. Today, as russet-red forest monarchs, they dwarf mankind and his fleeting existence.

Lord of these dendroid kings is the General Sherman Tree of Sequoia National Park's Giant Forest. This splendid Sequoiandendron giganteum has ruled over his mountain throneroom of giants, across from the Great Divide of the grand Sierra escarpment, for well over 2,000 years.

General Sherman's dimensions are difficult to comprehend. Several species of trees outlive his kind. One has a greater diameter. Three are known to grow taller. None is larger. In volume of total wood he stands alone as the largest living thing on the planet. At 275 feet tall, his awesome red profile is 36.5 feet thick (wider than many city streets). Estimates place the weight of his trunk alone at 1,385 tons! Were this titanic tree reduced into so many board feet of lumber there would be enough building material to construct a village of 40 five-room houses.

General Sherman's longevity is attributed to the fact that, like other giant sequoias, he is cloaked in a thick, tannin-rich bark which protects him against insects, fungi, and fire. Spongy and fibrous, nearly two feet thick at places, he is thus shielded from the elements like no other species of tree on earth. This extraordinary adaptation was well demonstrated recently when lightning struck the top of a sequoia giant in Yosemite National Park, during a July thunderstorm. The great tree's crown smoldered away quietly, without any apparent damage being done, until October, when a snowstorm extinguished the fire. About the only things that can seriously threaten a mature giant sequoia are severe climactic changes, earthquakes, serious erosion, or any other such combination of circumstances that might cause the great forest king to topple over.

Once fallen, these giants may lie intact on the forest floor for hundreds of years without showing any signs of decay.

Truly the giant sequoia of the Sierra Nevada represents a life form that approaches perfection.

occurs. Two thousand foot deep Little Yosemite Valley and the Illioutte Drainage on the south side merge with 4,000 foot Tenaya Canyon on the north. The floor of the Yosemite itself sits at an elevation of about 4,000 feet above sea level while her surrounding uplands soar to altitudes ranging from 7,000 to 8,000 feet.

Between the three branch chasms at the head of the Valley these uplands continue, blanketed with a dense forest of pine and fir. Occasionally they are themselves surmounted by isolated domes of granite.

Not one of the numerous vales and glades that drain into the Yosemite from this surrounding high country slopes to the bottom of that noble valley. On the contrary, each descends at a gentle gradient until it reaches the rim of the great excavation. There, terminated abruptly, these "hanging valleys," as geologists call them, empty their snow melt from such lofty heights in spectacular displays of leaping waterfalls and cascades. A phenomena relatively rare in nature, these free falling cataracts are among the highest and most spectacular in the world. Thus, as throughout the world famed Yellowstone National Park has become synonymous with geysers, so the Yosemite has come to stand for waterfalls.

Sharing both the name and the fame of the Valley, grand Yosemite Falls forms a perfect example of the Sierra's magnificent "hanging valleys." From a modest slope amidst the uplands of the Valley's northside, Yosemite Creek winds its way through the woods. Suddenly, suspended in midair by the stupendous walls of the great Valley, it plummets 2,425 feet to the floor of the chasm below. This awesome descent is composed of several phases. The great Upper Fall, the lesser or Lower Fall and an intermediate chain of cascades combine to form the single most breath-taking free leaping waterfall in the world, rivaled only by Venezuela's Angel Falls for supremacy as the world's highest.

In reality, however, the Yosemite region abounds with similar displays that surpass in height even this grand fall. Yet, because of the small volume of mountain streams that form their headwaters, each of these contenders exists only briefly as spring runoffs send shimmering veils, or ribbons, fluttering over the rim of the valley. Six hundred foot Tenaya Cascade, at the head of Tenaya Canyon is among these many temporary "ribbon" falls. Being the most voluminous, however, it deserves recognition among the great falls of the Yosemite, as does 1,612 foot high Ribbon Fall whose display, as it scintillates over the valley wall, gives rise to the highest, albeit briefest, free falling waterfall in the region.

In late spring and early summer such displays are innumerable as runoff from the high country snow mass fills upland streams and rivers to the verge of overflowing.

The "hanging valley" of Bridalveil Creek, major drainage system for the southern uplands, does not end as abruptly at the brink of the Yosemite. Ancient glaciers and high country runoff has carved out a V-shaped canyon that projects out over a mile into the Valley floor. Like an immense chute, lying low in the landscape, its funneled waters glide with amazing velocity down a steep gorge. Suddenly, the rushing torrent leaps out over a 620 foot precipice to form graceful Bridalveil Fall.

BRIDALVEIL FALLS

Suspended in spray, this splendid display rivals that of similar waterfalls in Switzerland. Surpassing all contenders by the beauty of its setting, however, Bridalveil is by far among the most remarkable waterfalls in the world. At dusk the cascade of this graceful fall is accompanied by a downward rush of chilled high country air. Such disturbance, emanating from the gulch of Bridalveil Creek, causes trees and shrubbery about the fall's base to sway erratically. This striking phenomena unquestionably accounts for the Indian name of the cataract, "fall of the puffing winds."

The successive falls of the Merced River itself, as it descends from Little Yosemite Valley, form the steps of a giant stairway hewn in stone. From Glacier Point, on the south side of Yosemite Valley, this natural causeway may best be viewed in its entirety. The uppermost step, from which Nevada Fall drops, is 600 feet high. The next step, giving rise to the turbulent whitewater of Diamond Cascades, is about 50 feet high. The lowermost step is graced by a broad curtain of water, 317 feet high, known as famous Vernal Fall. Altogether their combined total drop is more that 1,200 feet in a distance of little more than half a mile. Hiking up this giant's "stairway," along the "Mist Trail" to the top of Nevada Fall constitutes one of Yosemite's most popular attractions. Enroute one catches a glimpse of 370 foot Illioutte Fall, or Hidden Fall. Another fascinating display emanating from a little known "hanging valley," its waters disappear abruptly, thundering into the dark abyss of a well-timbered granite gorge.

In Tenaya Canyon, above picturesque Mirror Lake, the icy falls and cascades of Snow Creek tumble from their "hanging valley," draining yet another quarter of the high Sierra. In a total descent of over 2,000 feet, they cut a gorge through forested declivities that can best be viewed from atop Half Dome.

Elsewhere in the range, Rainbow Fall on the middle fork of the San Joaquin River, south of famed Devil's Postpile, makes a single leap of 150 feet on a cliff of columnar basalt to form a perfect white water curtain. Volcano Fall near the headwaters of the Kern River and Grizzly Fall in famed Kings Canyon are among countless notable cascades and cataracts that adorn the gorges and troughs of the grand Sierra Nevada.

Silent in mannerism, yet nonetheless exquisite, are the thousands of lakes that adorn the high Sierra. Catchment basins for rain and snow melt, they range in size from small ponds no more than 20 feet across to the spectacular Lake Tahoe, 21 miles long and 11 miles wide with a reported depth of 1,645 feet.

Glorious snowfields drape the purple-grey bulwark of the Sierra Nevada throughout much of the year. It was precisely this apparel that gave rise to the name of the range itself – Spanish terms signifying a snow covered, saw-toothed chain of mountains.

Water then, in all its forms, is the crowning glory of these great mountains. Be it in the magnificent profusion and variety of expressive waterfalls that leap from Yosemite's lofty cliffs or the hundreds of silent rock-bound lakes that adorn its high country, the waters of the Sierra are among the great escarpment's most superlative features. Above all, they

YOSEMITE FALLS

contribute to human welfare not only by virtue of their inspiring displays and serene settings but by supplying lifegiving sustenance to a West Coast population that today numbers in excess of 24 million.

HALF DOME

 he Sierra Nevada, together with its unparalleled Yosemite Valley, owes its unique ranking among the high country of the world to the splendor and variety of its geographic features. Sculpted and weathered, it harbors a wealth of monumental rock masses and granite formations that stand unrivaled for both beauty and sheer numbers by any other creation on earth.

The cliffs of Yosemite stand remarkably sheer, at vertical angles. Indeed the scenic character of the Valley itself is not merely due to its great depth and unusual form but to the distinctive sculpture of these walls.

El Capitan reigns preeminent among the Sierra's massive granite formations. This great cliff – the most majestic in the Yosemite, and perhaps in the world, – rises from the valley in so clean a line that its height is peculiarly difficult to evaluate at a glance. First estimates by those who camped at its foot now seem ludicrous. As Dr. Bummell, chronicler of Yosemite's discovery, relates in his report, "one official estimated El Capitan at 400 feet, Captain Boeling at 800 feet . . . My estimate was a sheer perpendicularity of at least 1,500 feet." Trigonometric measurements made later during the first official state survey of the Valley determined the height of the cliff to be fully 3,000 feet; its dome-shaped crown above the brow rising yet another 500 feet.

Across from El Capitan stands the ponderous gathering of stones known as Cathedral Rocks. This gigantic formation projects more than a mile out onto the floor of the valley, creating Yosemite's most narrow profile. Here three summits, carved from a single asymmetric ridge, loom one above another in an ascending series. Towering above the valley, they stand 1,650, 2,590 and 2,680 feet in height respectively. On the west side, Cathedral Rocks slopes evenly to the gulch through which the waters of Bridalveil Creek race to the precipice of Bridalveil Fall.

In the embayment east of Cathedral Rocks, in marked contrast to such solid figures, stands two slender, tapering shafts known as the Cathedral Spires. Frailest of all rock formations in the Valley, they rise to heights of 2,160 and 950 feet.

Along the north wall stand famed Three Brothers, named in remembrance of the sons of Yosemite's last tribal chieftain. These gabled forms, each rising above the other at the same angle, represent the finest of asymmetric sculpture in all of the Sierra Nevada.

Further up the Valley, Sentinel Rock stands forth from the south wall, like an obelisk, with sheer front and sharp, splintered top. At 7,038 feet in height the Sentinel dominates a commanding view of this high country throne room. So splendid is its form and positioning that the Ahwahneechee (or Uhumati, anglicized to Yosemite, and meaning Grizzly Bear) Indians spoke of it as if it were a god; a great spirit embodied in stone who watched over their mountain home.

FINEST OF ASYMMETRIC SCULPTURE in all of the Sierra Nevada, the Three Brothers (left) tower above Yosemite Valley.

WILLIAM NEILL

BASKET DOME

MAJESTIC HALF DOME (right).

Most remarkable among Yosemite's rock forms are those which cluster above the head of the Valley. Directly across from Glacier Point are the Royal Arches, a series of immense natural curvatures carved in bas-relief on a wall 1,500 feet high. Flanking them, much like a corner post, at the mouth of Tenaya Canyon is Washington Column, a colossal 1,700 foot granite pillar. Surmounting the Arches is the smoothly rounded, helmet-shaped mass known as North Dome. A short distance beyond sits Basket Dome, a similar yet smaller symmetrical formation.

Dome-shaped features abound in the Upper Yosemite. Sentinel Dome, southwest of Glacier Point, is among the most visible. Mount Starr King, rising east of Illioutte Ridge forms the highest such feature in the entire region.

To this general category of domes one might include both Liberty Cap and Mount Broderick, two bastions of stone that frame Little Yosemite Valley. Honorable mention should be made of the rounded-back Mount Watkins, most recollected for its impressive reflected image in the ever-receding waters of Mirror Lake.

Unquestionably the most remarkable of all stone monuments, not only in the Yosemite but in the Sierra itself, is majestic Half Dome. Planted as if on a pedestal, it raises its imperious form above the divide between Tenaya Canyon and Little Yosemite Valley. Rounded on the south side and cut off sheer on north, it gives the appearance of a great dome split asunder; its one half having been completely destroyed. Nearly a mile long and a quarter of a mile broad it rises 4,748 feet about the floor of Yosemite Valley, the Matterhorn of the Range of Light.

Only one eminence in the Yosemite overshadows Half Dome. At an altitude if 9,929 feet the great billowy formations of Cloud's Rest stretch more than two miles across and a mile high. A lofty ridge northeast of the famed Half Dome hallmark, Cloud's Rest is one of the greastest unbroken fronts of bare rock in the entire Sierra Nevada, and therefore in the world.

Beyond Cloud's Rest stretches the endless panorama of the true high Sierra, with its myriad outcroppings and sawtooth peaks. Within the confines of Yosemite National Park such grandeur culminates in glacier-shrouded Mount Lyell. Here one encounters mountains of another color, some sporting brilliant red tones while others appear a somber black. These contrasting high country peaks are remnants of a far more ancient landscape, one which surmounted the great block of granite before it was forced upward to form the Sierra Nevada. Eroded away through millions of years of assault by the forces of nature, they are all that remains of an ancient land once inhabited by dinosaurs.

Along the eastern face of the granite escarpment, prehistoric volcanic activity further colored the range with pumice and ash. Most extraordinary among these monuments of volcanism is the Devil's Postpile,a 60 foot perpendicular wall of octagonally shaped basalt unrivaled in the perfection of its geometric form.

From Mono Lake south to Mammoth Mountain and then again near Owens Valley stretch more than 30 volcanic craters.

(continued on page 40)

DICK ROWAN

With no written language, the Ahwahneechee (Yosemite) Indians became master storytellers. During cold winter months they would gather around a warm fire and school their children in the verbal history of their people. This living legacy, passed down from one generation to the next, provided a certain continuity to tribal leadership and a sense of belonging to each individual. Such yarns far transcended their values as a source of mere entertainment. Each related elements of the Ahwahneechee's value system, their philosophy of life, their traditions. In an endearing, child-like, yet wise fashion, these tales attempted to interpret and explain the mysteries of nature. Two popular anecdotes, the legend of El Capitan and the origins of Half Dome, illustrate the refined degree of skill to which this imaginative and practical method of teaching had been developed among these early people. They are as follows . . .

THE LEGEND OF HALF DOME

Long ago in Ahwahnee (Yosemite) there were many bird and animal people. One of them went to Mono Lake and married an Indian Woman named Tis-sa-ack. He started to bring his bride back to Ahwahnee to live.

The husband carried a roll of deer skins on his back and held a staff in his hand. Tis-sa-ack had a baby cradle in her arms and a pointed carrying basket on her back.

When the travelers came to where Mirror Lake is now, the new husband quarreled with Tis-sa-ack. She wanted him to return with her and live at Mono Lake. He said that there were no oaks or other trees there. Said she, "I will take acorns and seeds along and we can plant trees." But her husband would not listen to her plea.

Finally Tis-sa-ack began to cry and ran back along the trail. Then the husband became angry. He cut a green limb and ran after his run-away wife, beating her severely.

Tis-sa-ack threw the carrying basket at him. This basket turned to stone and became Basket Dome. Still running, Tis-sa-ack threw the baby cradle at her husband. It also turned to stone and became the Royal Arches.

Because they had profaned the Ahwahnee with their anger, both Tis-sa-ack and her husband were also turned to stone. The husband became North Dome, and the wife became Half Dome (Mono women bob their hair and cut it in bangs. Half Dome looks just like the head and shoulders of a Mono woman.).

Since the quarrel, Tis-sa-ack has always been sorry. The old Indians say that the tears she shed formed Mirror Lake. You can still see the marks of these tears where they ran down the face of Tis-sa-ack (Half Dome).

ED COOPER

THE LEGEND OF EL CAPITAN

Long, long ago, there lived, in the valley of Ahwahnee two bear cubs. One hot summer day they slipped away from their mother and went down to the river for a swim. When they came out of the water, they were so tired that they lay down to rest on an immense, flat boulder and fell fast asleep. As they slumbered, the huge rock began to rise slowly until, at length, it towered into the blue sky far above the tree tops, and woolly, white clouds fell over the sleeping cubs like fleecy coverlets.

The distraught mother bear searched in vain for her two cubs. Although she questioned every animal in the valley, not one could give her a clue as to the whereabouts of her children. At last To-tah-khan, the sharp-eyed crane, discovered them still asleep on top of the great rock. Then the mother bear became more anxious than ever lest her cubs should awaken and feel so frightened upon finding themselves up near the blue sky that they would jump off and be killed.

All the other animals in the valley felt very sorry for the mother bear and promised to help rescue the cubs. Gathering together, each attempted to climb the great rock, but it was slippery as glass, and their feet would not hold.

When all had given up, along came the tiny measuring worm. "I believe I can climb up to the top and bring the cubs down," it courageously announced.

The other animals all sneered and made sport of this boast from one of the most insignificant of their number, but the measuring worm paid no attention to their insults and immediately began the perilous ascent. "Too-tack, too-tack, To-takan-oo-lah," it chanted, and its feet clung even to that polished surface. Higher and higher it went until the animals below began to realize that the measuring worm was not so stupid after all.

Weak and exhausted, it reached the top of the great rock at last, awakened the cubs, and miraculouly guided them safely down to their anxious mother. All the animals were overjoyed with the return of the cubs and loudly sang the praises of the measuring worm. As a token of honor the animals decided to name the great rock "To-to-kan-oo-lah" for the brave little measuring worm.

ED COOPER

THE GOLDEN TROUT

NATIVE TO THE WATERS OF THE SIERRA NEVADA ARE THREE SPECIES OF TROUT; AMONG THEM THE GOLDEN, ACCLAIMED BY MANY TO BE THE MOST BEAUTIFUL FRESH-WATER FISH IN THE WORLD. SPORTING ALL THE BRILLIANCE IN COLORING OF ITS TROPICAL COUNTERPARTS, THE GOLDEN HAS BEEN TRANSPLANTED FROM ITS NATIVE HABITAT IN THE SOUTHERN SIERRA TO PONDS, STREAMS, AND LAKES THROUGHOUT THE RANGE BY ENTHUSIASTIC FISHERMAN.

Today, surrounded by miles of pinkish-red to dark grey lava flows, they add an eerie primeval aspect to the otherwise contemporary western American scene.

Each of the aforementioned rock forms are of distinctive character, wholly different from rock features commonly found in canyons and mountain valleys throughout the world. Even among sister valleys of the Sierra Nevada, which are carved of the same granite rock by the same forces of nature, the Yosemite's singular vast array of stone splendor maintains its preeminence. For, while King's Canyon, Hetch Hetchy, Tehipite, and other Sierra chasms sport granite or volcanic oddities, none can surpass this one spectacular Valley with its innumerable examples of extraordinary features.

Although more conspicuous throughout the Sierra Nevada than is typically the case in a mountain range, these frowning stone battlements nonetheless are softened here and there by ancient woodlands and superlative primeval forests. It is along the middle slope of the western escarpment that such growth reaches its zenith, although noble stands along the eastern face of the range are quite as impressive with their climax forests of yellow pine.

It is, in fact, the yellow pine (ponderosa and jeffrey being principal among its members) and the beautiful sugar pine that form the most extensive groves here in one of California's premiere timberlands. Highly prized commercially for their straight beams and broad, clear boards, they have been recklessly "harvested" from much of the range. In fact, most stands of yellow pine in the Sierra Nevada today are second growth forests; trees which have matured on lands previously decimated by unregulated logging activities.

Below the timber belt, the digger pine gains preeminence in a land otherwise dominated by oak. At higher altitudes the lodgepole pine is most common.

Along the precipitous eastern extent of the range, foxtail and whitebark pine, often twisted and stunted by harsh weather conditions, afford beauty and modest shelter. Their weather-beaten forms survive sub-arctic conditions to dress stark stone ramparts.

The pinyon pine, common throughout most of the Southwest, is a rare sight in the Sierra. Found only along the eastern wall, it is easily identifiable by its peculiar arrangement of needles (one per socket, where as most pines sport two, three, or five per socket) and its highly prized pine nuts. The latter, esteemed as a delicacy, come well deserved to those with the patience to force the tiny kernels from the trees' hardy cones.

Douglas fir and mountain hemlock grace the more well-watered extensions of the range, particularly in the north, as does western pine and incense cedar (often mistaken for the giant sequoia because of its texture and coloring). White fir and red fir constitute a great deal of the forest belt along its uppermost boundary. Beyond, on rocky slopes and plateaus, the tenacious juniper, an uncompromising individualist, clings to life in an inhospitable world.

In autumn high country passes and eastern facing slopes are brilliantly colored as groves of aspen are magically transformed into shimmering forests of gold. Elsewhere, canyon walls and valley floors are set ablaze with the crimson and auburn of bigleaf maple and water birch.

Dogwood adorns the Sierra in spring with fabulous displays of graceful white petals. Indeed, during spring and throughout the summer the Sierra Nevada is transformed into one great garden of flowers.

Fragrant azaleas greet visitors to the Yosemite, their white blossoms, mixed with bright yellow evening primrose, create unforgettable displays.

Amidst the towering giants of the forest belt one encounters the beautiful little mariposa lily. Varying in color from lavender to celestial white, each petal is conspicuously marked by a terra cotta eyespot.

In the high country, meadows are dressed with a galaxy of pink shooting stars, blue gentian, and red, Indian paintbrush.

Higher still, in the heather above timberline, the Sierra primrose, scarlet gilia, the rose-purple bryanthus and dainty white bells of Cassiope create colorful alpine garden displays.

Throughout the range varieties of lupine dress the landscape in shades that vary from blue and white to yellow.

Of the more than ten thousand species of insects found in the Sierra it is the butterfly that remains the most conspicuous, adding a subtle touch of color and fantasy to this mammoth landscape of granite mountains and tall timber. Floating and dancing in glade and meadow, like imaginary sprites, they remind the adventurer not to overlook the intricacies of a delicate ecosystem frequently overshadowed by 14,000 foot peaks and valleys six to 8,000 feet deep.

Wildlife abounds throughout the Sierra Nevada. Subjection to man's encroachment began when California's gold rush brought the world rushing in. Forty-niners instigated wanton slaughter amidst such abundance, bringing about the demise of many species of big game. Today some animals have made a dramatic comeback. Others tenaciously teeter at the brink of extinction, officially registered as having already succumbed to oblivion.

The grizzly bear, emblazoned on California's state flag, is one such notable case in point. Largest and most ferocious of Sierra mammals, a mature California grizzly may span more than ten feet in length. Easily distinguished from the more diminutive, and less aggressive, black bear by its large shoulder hump, long front claws, and color of pelage, the monstrous beast often weighs more than 1,000 pounds, with undocumented reports claiming 2,000 pound specimens. The grizzly's brute strength and general lack of fear posed a serious threat to early miners, settlers, and ranchers. For half a century this most noble of North American big game was subjected to ruthless, often unwarranted, slaughter.

The last official report of a grizzly sighting in the Sierra Nevada occurred at Sequoia National Park in 1924. Neverthe-

MULES EAR

(continued on page 44)

The Bear, the Fly and the Grasshopper *

July 21. - Sketching on the Dome - no rain; saw a common house fly and a grasshopper and a brown bear. The fly and grasshopper paid me a merry visit on the top of the Dome, and I paid a visit to the bear in the middle of a small garden meadow between the Dome and the camp. I was anxious to get a good look at the sturdy mountaineer without alarming him; so drawing myself up noiselessly back of one of the largest of the trees I peered past its bulging buttresses, exposing only a part of my head, and there stood neighbor Bruin within a stone's throw, his hips covered by tall grass and flowers, and his front feet on the trunk of a Fir that had fallen out into the meadow, which raised his head so high that he seemed to be standing erect. He had not yet seen me, but was looking and listening attentively, showing that in some way he was aware of my appproach. I watched his gestures and tried to make the most of my opportunity to learn what I could about him, fearing he would catch sight of me and run away. For I had been told that this sort of bear, the cinnamon, always ran from his bad brother man, never showing fight unless wounded or in defense of young. He made a telling picture standing alert in the sunny forest garden. How well he played his part, harmonizing in bulk and color and shaggy hair with the trunks of the trees and lush vegetation, as natural a feature as any other in the landscape. After examining at leisure, I thought I should like to see his gait in running, so I made a sudden rush at him, shouting and swinging my hat to frighten him, expecting to see him make haste to get away. But to my dismay he did not run or show any sign of running. On the contrary, he stood his ground ready to fight and defend himself, lowered his head, thrust it forward, and looked sharply and fiercely at me. Then I suddenly began to fear that upon me would fall the work of running; but I was afraid to run, and therefore, like the bear, held my ground. We stood staring at each other in solemn silence within a dozen yards or thereabouts, while I fervently hoped that the power of the human eye over wild beasts would prove as great as it is said to be. How long our awfully strenuous interview lasted, I don't know; but at length in the slow fullness of time he pulled his huge paws down off the log, and with magnificent deliberation turned and walked leisurely up the meadow, stopping frequently to look back over his shoulder to see whether I was pursuing him, then moving on again, evidently neither fearing me very much nor trusting me. He was probably about five hundred pounds in weight, a broad rusty bundle of ungovernable wildness, a happy fellow whose lines have fallen in pleasant places. The flowery glade in which I saw him so well framed like a picture, is one of the best of all I have yet discovered. Tall lilies were swinging their bells over the bear's back, with geraniums, larkspurs, columbines, and daisies brushing against his sides. A place for angels, one would say, instead of bears.

*(Taken from the journal of John Muir; written during his first summer in the Sierra).

TOM McHUGH

CALIFORNIA GRIZZLY

AMERICAN BLACK BEAR

less, and off the record, isolated incidents attributed to *Ursus Arctos Californicus* (California grizzly), as well as rare undocumented sightings by knowledgeable backpackers and hunters, keep the legend of the great beast alive.

Similar folklore and history surround the mountain jaguar, a beast rare even prior to the days of the gold rush. Then, like the grizzly, as a predator and threat to human life, it faced extinction at the hands of ruthless hunters. Its threat more contrived than factual, last reported sightings of the spotted, leopard-like cat occurred south of the range above Palm Springs in 1929.

At the time of Kit Carson's arrival in California, around 1840, herds of Tule elk numbering in the hundreds of thousands grazed the foothills and lowlands surrounding the western Sierra. Smallest of the elk family, their noble carriage (bulls sporting magnificent antlers) formed a splendid sight as they roamed en masse across the steppes and marshes. Hunted off to feed hungry miners, their range was subsequently converted into farmland. Today representative herds grace the shores of Owens Lake along the Eastern Sierra south of Bishop. Isolated reserves exist, scattered on both sides of the great range. Fortunately the regal animal is making a slow but steady comeback from a remnant herd that numbered less than one hundred members.

Not as fortunate was the fleet pronghorn antelope whose numbers once rivaled those of the elk in populations adjoining both sides of the Sierra range. Today it is no more.

Rare, yet intrepid too, is the Sierra Bighorn, a close relative to the Rocky Mountain Bighorn. At the turn of the century bands of these majestic animals roamed the crest of the high Sierra. Competing with invading herds of domesticated sheep and unrelenting hunting, the bighorn population was seriously threatened. Today small isolated family groups persist, primarily in the high country of the southern range.

Other species of big game have been more fortunate. The black bear, too common according to many campers who've had their food supplies and equipment invaded by marauders, roams over the entire length of the range. Though substantially smaller and far less dangerous than cousin grizzly, the black bear does pose a threat to personal safety. Government agencies have gone to considerable length to keep people and bears separated, thus avoiding injuries or harm to either man or bear. Although so named, black bears are often brown or cinnamon in color. Their antics are a delight to behold, but should always be enjoyed from a safe distance.

The panther, or mountain lion, too is still prevalent in the Sierra Nevada. Nocturnal and extremely fearful of man this beautiful animal is rarely seen by the millions who briefly pass through the mountains each year.

The colorful wildcat, or bobcat, is somewhat more conspicuous, his dusky coat sometimes taking on an amber, almost orange color. Much smaller than the mountain lion, which often exceeds 6 feet from nose to tip of tail, the wildcat is famed for his nerve-wracking scream, rarely heard and far less threatening than presumed.

Wolves, although reported in early travelers' accounts, have never inhabited California. With the possible exception of a "stray" from farther east, most sightings have turned out to be none other than the Mountain Coyote. Another animal famed for its voice, the coyote has haunted many a camper in the wilderness with its midnight serenading.

Outnumbering all other large mammals in the range, Mule Deer grace virtually every glen and meadow throughout the Sierra Nevada.

Most dangerous of Sierra denizens, excluding the legendary grizzly, is the Wolverine. This bear-like member of the weasel family is nocturnal and a loner by nature. With the exception of a brief social interlude during the mating season (February through March), it maintains a solitary lifestyle. Wolverines are vicious fighters. They will prey upon deer and have been know to attack both bear and mountain lion.

Fishers, otter, mink, pine martin, red fox, raccoon, skunk, marmots, and a variety of squirrels and rabbits add to the color and spectacle of life in the highlands. As most of the range today remains under some sort of reserve or other protected status, nature lovers are hopeful that all species once found here will continue to regain their preeminence and flourish.

eologists today believe that some sixty million years ago the entire Sierra region was a coastal lowland sporting lush tropical vegetation. Early during that era of earth's history known as the Tertiary Period, successive uplifts, destined to become the Sierra Nevada, began to occur. Massive continental plates collided, forcing a western contender skyward as its eastern assailant was pushed downward. The high Sierra thus appeared, bowed into an asymmetric arch of ever-increasing height. At first the uplift attained only a moderate elevation, yet even at this early stage it betrayed the westward slant that today is one of this range's most striking features. By the end of that Tertiary Period, about 20 million years ago, the Sierra had risen several thousand feet, its slant correspondingly steepened.

With the dawning of the Quaternary Period, the great Sierra escarpment had assumed its present stature, primarily that of a tremendous block tilted eastward at great height.

As the Ice Age began, basins along the eastern wall of the Sierra sank, filling with runoff from the great glaciers that had begun to form along an alpine crest. Most watershed, however, continued draining southwestward, each river running roughly parallel to the other as dictated by the gently sloping western flanks of the new range. Thus was the course of the Merced established and the position of Yosemite Valley determined.

The Merced is what geologists refer to as a "superimposed" river. Most other streams, emanating from the Sierra and coursing their way across its western flank are not unlike the Merced. Herein lies a clue as to the origin of Yosemite and its many sister valleys. Each of the Sierra's capacious U-shaped

(continued on page 48)

MOUNTAIN LION

MULE DEER

KARIN HARRISON

concavities seems to occur in areas dominated by fractured rocks. Agents of erosion have worked away here untrammeled with comparative facility down through the ages.

The cutting of canyons by rivers was an inevitable consequence, as the tilting of the Sierra block pushed its crestline ever skyward. The slope of a stream thus steepened, its flow was accelerated. Each proceeded to entrench itself faster and faster, vigorously cutting away at its bed. In the process, canyons or valleys were created, the floors of which lay at ever lower levels.

Such newly formed valleys, carved thus from what had previously been the floor of earlier valleys, are tremendously significant formations in the Sierra landscape. With the aid of a trained student of land forms, one can reconstruct, in imagination, the original parameters of what once was the Yosemite. Even her exquisite waterfalls reveal critical clues that lead to an understanding of the Sierra Nevada's evolution.

Standing atop the summit of El Capitan, and looking westward, one sees that the long, even-topped profile of a very ancient and very shallow valley is outlined.

Below this ancient valley appear the much better preserved features of a somewhat narrower valley. This valley within a valley was fully 1,500 feet deep, yet it was also characterized by a broad fairly level floor, as is evidenced by many remaining flats and undulating surfaces. One of these, Big Meadow, a few miles northeast of El Portal, is a highly visible remnant of this old second-valley floor.

Remarkably, a third V-shaped gorge, that through which the Merced flows today, has been excavated from the second valley, creating a "three-story" profile. What is commonly and loosely referred to as the Merced Canyon then, is actually a steep-walled inner gorge cut into the floor of a spacious old valley, which in turn lies itself within a broad valley of even greater antiquity. Such three-story configurations are characteristic of the Tuolumne, San Joaquin and countless other river gorges that traverse the range.

WILLIAM NEILL

BROAD-VALLEY STAGE

MOUNTAIN-VALLEY STAGE

CANYON STAGE

John Muir was the first to reconstruct this primeval scenario. In the beginning it appears as if the Yosemite, then as now, was a broadly open, level-floored valley flanked by rolling hills and occasional ridges. Through this gentle landscape meandered the Merced. The crown of El Capitan rose in gentle curves to a height of 900 feet, revealing little more than its present brow. Half Dome, a massive, irregular looking bulk, reared its summit 500 feet above the lay of the land. Curvaceous and undulating, there were no angular formations; no pinnacles or cliffs. Even the Cathedral Rocks appeared as nothing more than massive, rounded knobs sloping gradually to the valley floor.

Neither was this landscape graced by capricious waterfalls or cascades. All tributary streams flowed, uninterrupted, into the placid waters of the Merced. Densely forested with tropical verdure, the Yosemite even then, hidden behind its primeval mask, must have been glorious to behold; its expansive floor grazed over by herds of strange beasts long since extinct.

The crestline of the high Sierra appeared much as it does today, having already been pushed skyward by colliding plates and buckling action beneath its great granite block. Yet, the sawtooth nature of its modern profile had not yet been assumed. Full bodied and rounded, not yet sculpted by rain, wind and ice, it created a far different configuration then that which strikes awe within us today. Gentle shoulders and benches flanked regions that were destined to be numbered among the most spectacular canyon gorges on earth.

Great uplifts pushed the Sierra higher during the Tertiary Period causing the Merced (and other rivers) to accelerate canyon-cutting processes. Abandoning its meandering habit, it wore away at the valley floor, creating a deep, walled labyrinth. By the end of the Pliocene, some ten million years ago, it had entrenched itself almost a thousand feet.

In the Yosemite, tributaries were unable to cut away as rapidly as the Merced. Provided with substantially less watershed, hence less cutting power, they found themselves left hanging at greater and greater heights above the main drainage system. No sharp rims defined the edges of Yosemite's uplands, yet monoliths were beginning to assume their awesome dimensions, rising several thousand feet above the eroded causeway. Woodlands became accentuated by rugged crags and palisades. Bridalveil Creek, not yet a free falling waterfall, emptied into this new Yosemite near where the lip of its chute now appears, raging on its steep, but not seared off, course to join the ever-accelerating Merced. Yosemite overall had thus assumed the dimensions of a great canyon.

About a million years ago cool, drying trends gave way to a cold and violent chill. Thus began the Great Ice Age. In the upper valleys of the Range of Light snow gathered to depths of thousands of feet, becoming compacted into sheets of ice – glaciers. Tongue-shaped, they inched their way down the canyons of the Merced, Tuolumne, San Joaquin, and others, superseding the streams as valley-cutting agents.

Geologists today estimate that not one but four such Ice Age assaults, interrupted by periods of relative warmth, during which glaciers melted only to form again, carved away at the canyons of the Sierra Nevada. Each glacial stage superimposed its changes on those wrought previously, further wearing away at canyon walls, grinding valley floors and polishing domes and towers.

When at last the great reign of ice came to an end, less than ten thousand years ago, Yosemite Valley no longer presented the appearance of a narrow "three-story" canyon. Both downward and sideways the glaciers had quarried; trimming off projectiles, cutting back the craggy slopes of the pre-Ice Age river canyon, to reveal sheer, smooth cliffs. Cascades had been transformed into their present free falling forms of astounding grace and height. Throughout the length of the valley the inner gorge of the Merced had been wiped out. In its stead was the broadly concave basin floor that greets us today, though not yet visible. The spacious trough, filled by glacial melt, was now Lake Yosemite.

FIRST GLACIAL STAGES

LAST GLACIAL STAGE

LAKE STAGE

51

ED COOPER

With time the waters receded. Extensive park-like meadows appeared. As recently as one hundred years ago, comparatively little invasion of the timber belt had occurred, leaving grasslands that dwarf even today's expansive settings.

Great cliffs and domes throughout the Sierra consist of massive granite. El Capitan and Cathedral Rocks stand out boldly from the Valley walls because they are made up of enormous monoliths that would not yield to the onslaught of glaciers. Half Dome, and other Sierra formations, rise high in the landscape. Their unfractured masses have survived the destruction brought on by climactic extremes; yet they owe their smoothly rounded forms not only to the grinding of overriding glaciers – some of them were never so overridden – but to the curious bursting of concentric layers, or "shells," from their surfaces as well; a process known as exfoliation.

Subtle remnants of great glaciers abound throughout the Yosemite. Huge "erratic" boulders, perched precariously atop ridges and hillsides, bare witness to the rivers of ice that, when melted, left each great stone where it now sits. Looking peculiarly out of place, solitary erratics frequently adorn mirror-like slopes polished by overriding glaciers. Piles of debris, known as glacial moraine, lie scattered about the mouths of canyons where receding ice flows discharged them thousands of years ago. Now overgrown by forest, they remain, nevertheless, clearly visible to the keen eye.

The Merced today continues to deepen its canyon. Cliffs are further sculpted by frost, heat and rain. Of Yosemite's rocky titans, National Geographic's Ross Bennett wrote "they still stand – immovable, majestic, their feet among the flowers." Yet, even El Capitan, seemingly as eternal as the "Rock of Ages" itself, is nonetheless continually subjected to almost imperceptible changes. Yosemite may well last forever but it will forever be in a state of metamorphosis.

ERRATIC BOULDER

THE EFFECTS OF GLACIATION are visible throughout Yosemite, where smooth, polished, dome-shaped configurations, such as those viewed from Olmstead Point (preceding pages) along Tioga Road, and at El Capitan (left), abound.

WILLIAM NEILL

©1985 MUSEUM OF FINE ARTS, BOSTON

VALLEY OF THE YOSEMITE BY ALBERT BIERSTADT (1830-1902)

MISSION SAN CARLOS
BORROMEO, ESTABLISHED
AT CARMEL IN 1770

FRANCISCAN PADRES PER-
FORM THE FIRST BAPTISM
IN ALTA CALIFORNIA

Spanish colonization of Alta California had begun long before European exploration uncovered El Dorado's great eastern wall. With settlements and mission outposts confined to the coast, New Spain's vast interior remained an unmapped mystery.

It was the plight of the American Indian that brought modern man firstly in contact with America's granite partition and secondly with her unrivaled Yosemite Valley.

In ancient times six distinct groups of Indians inhabited the region that we know today as California's Sierra Nevada. They were the Washoe and Paiute Indians of the east wall and the Maidu, Miwok, Monachi (Mono) and Yokuts of the western slope. Of these primitive nations it was the Yokuts who first came into contact with modern man.

Two centuries following the discovery of California, long after the genius and energy that had brought Spain to its zenith as a world power had expended itself, the declining Iberian empire instigated colonization of its last great frontier. Due in large measure to greatly exaggerated reports of Russian, British, and American invasions, King Philip V determined to establish a more visible presence on this, the furthest province of his world-girding empire.

Franciscan missionaries accompanied conquistadors on what was to become Spain's last great empire-building effort. Souls subdued by the sword were to find eternal salvation under the cross of Catholicism. A greatly embellished "epoch" in the history of the New World, this period of California mission building gave rise to perhaps the most nostalgic and romantic era in the development of America's Far West.

White-washed adobe and red-tiled outposts came to grace the golden hills and vales of coastal California. Campaniles rang out across El Dorado, heralding the advent of civilization and Christianity in a land little removed from the Stone Age.

On occasion missionaries, in company with soldiers of the Spanish Crown, set out to explore the great unknown that lie just beyond their narrow coastal thread of empire. These brief excursions were initially conducted in an effort to select mission sites and identify potential converts.

In 1772 Captain Pedro Fages, in company with Father Juan Crespi, came within sight of California's great Sierra mountains. It was the first time European eyes had beheld such granite grandeur. At the convergence of the Sacramento and San Joaquin Rivers Father Crespi records:

"We made out that these arms or three large rivers were formed by a very large river, a league in width at least, *which descended from some high mountains to the southeast, very far distant.*"

Later, additional insight was imparted that same year, when, enroute to the frontier outpost at San Diego, Fages again came within view of the great range. From a vantage point below Tejon Pass in the Tehachapi Range above Los Angeles, he described the splendid vista much as it appears today:

"The range inland on the other side of the river is very high and its peaks are perpetually covered with snow. Many trees

of a variety of species grow in the excellent soil of the foothills."

Thus, with the reports of Fages and Crespi, the great mountain range entered the annals of recorded history. Four years later, while searching for an overland route to link colonies in New Mexico with proposed settlements at San Francisco, Father Pedro Font, in company with Francisco Garcis, came upon and gave far-reaching attention to California's great stone rampart. On April 2, 1776 Font recorded, "Looking to the northeast from a point just south of Suisun Bay, we saw an immense treeless plain into which the water spreads widely, forming several low-islets; at the opposite end of this extensive plain, about 40 leagues off, we saw *a snow-covered mountain range* (un gran sierra nevada) which seemed to me to run from south-southeast to north-northeast." Although earlier sightings introduced the mammoth range, it was this report that most herald as the day when the Range of Light became a reality to the civilized world.

Thus, the great chain of mountains, by way of Font's report to the Crown, received far-reaching acclaim as well as a name, initially applied as purely descriptive and never intended as a proper sobriquet.

Not until 1805 did subjects of the Spanish sovereign attempt to penetrate this "Gran Sierra Nevada." During the interim it seems that California Indians had acquired a taste for horseflesh. Others, tired of subjection to a philosophy they could not understand, burned with a desire to return to their old ways. Thus, fleeing neophytes and marauding horse thieves from the Sierra foothills lured Spanish justice inland. Raids on Yokut camps rarely recovered more than equine skeletons. It was these adventures, carried out for the most part by Ensign Gabriel Moraga, however, that shed greater light upon New Spain's most prominent geographic feature. In defense of the Franciscan empire, Moraga invaded Iberia's rugged sanctuary in search of Indian runaways and thieves. His raids and subsequent explorations resulted in the effective identification and naming of many of the Sierra's great rivers. Among them the Kings (discovered on January 6, the day of Epiphany, and named for the Magi who brought gifts to the boy King Jesus), Merced (named for Virgin Mary, "Our Lady of Mercy"), and the Sacramento were charted. On one such expedition Moraga recorded, "looking to the northeast through a gap in the grove of the river bank, we discerned the famous Sierra Nevada. The white part of this Sierra seemed to be all snow, although as they say, it is also a species of white rock which looks like snow."

Slowly the nature and extent of the great range was ascertained, yet it remained to the Spanish a foreboding wilderness affording no clue as to the natural splendor hidden in its canyons or the wealth of gold lying exposed in its high country streams.

The spring of 1827 marked an event of great portent in the history of California. It was then that a fortuitous omen appeared upon the great Sierra divide in the personage of one Bible-toting mountain man by the name of Jedediah Strong

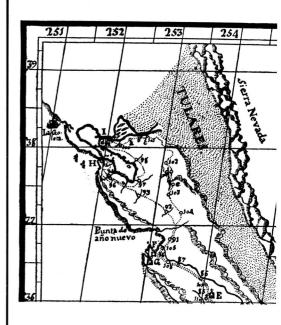

EARLIEST KNOWN MAP
OF THE SIERRA NEVADA

ENSIGN GABRIEL MORAGA (following page) whose many adventures resulted in the effective disclosure of the nature and extent of California's grand Sierra Nevada.

59

JEDEDIAH STRONG SMITH

Smith. His forced march across that great range signaled the beginning of the Americanization of El Dorado.

As a partner, working for the firm of Smith, Jackson and Sumner, Jed Smith, at age 27, struck out for the Pacific Coast in search of ever-elusive and highly-prized beaver pelts. Its Rocky Mountain domain having been greatly played out, Jedediah attempted to locate new populations in an effort to prolong the life of a dying fur trade. Entering coastal California from Cajon Pass (near Los Angeles) the unwary trapper was promptly arrested by a suspicious Mexican governor, at Mission San Gabriel. Upon being released, Smith and his party were ordered to leave what had, since rebellion with Spain, become Mexican territory by the same route which they had used to enter it. Having no intentions of abandoning his search, however, Jed headed back toward the desert from Los Angeles until out of town. Then, turning his face to the north, he continued, undaunted, upon his journey.

Though young, Jedediah had already gained a well earned reputation as one of the most experienced of an extraordinary group of "mountain men." Highly respected, not only for his physical prowess and frontier knowledge but for high moral character, a quality rare among his contemporaries, Smith would gain international acclaim for his illustrious, albeit brief, career in the Far West.

Born in New York, on January 6, 1799, Jedediah received a good education, well grounded in the scriptures. At the age of twenty-three he set out for St. Louis, center of the growing fur trade, to seek his fortune in the West. During the years that ensued he gained more knowledge and familiarity with terra incognita than that possessed by any other man of his day, only to have his career cut short in 1831 on the Cimarron by Indian arrows.

From Mission San Gabriel Smith records:

"I steared my course northwest, keeping from 150 to 200 miles from the sea coast, *a very high range of mountains, being on the east.* After traveling 300 miles in that direction, through a country somewhat fertile, in which there were a great many Indians . . . On my arrival at a river which I called the Wim-mee-che I found a few Beaver-Elk, Deer, and Antelope in abundance."

Threatened with incarceration again by Mexican authorities at San Jose, and having adequately ascertained that California lay well west of the beavers' principal domain, Smith decided that it was time to rejoin his comrades at Salt Lake. With no desire to repeat the long and risky trek back to Los Angeles, he searched for a way over the seemingly endless chain of mountains that had bordered his trail for so long. "I here made a small hunt and attempted to take my party across the mountains," he records, "to come on and join my partners at the Great Salt Lake. I found the snow so deep . . . that I could not cross my horses, five of which starved to death. I was compelled therefore to return to the valley which I had left, and there leaving my party I started with two men, seven horses, and two mules, which I loaded with hay for the horses and provisions for ourselves, and started on the twentieth of May and succeeded in crossing it in eight days, having lost only one mule. I found the snow on the top of the mountain from four to eight feet deep, but it was so consolidated by the heat of the sun that my horses only sunk from half a foot to one foot deep."

And so it was that the great mountains were conquered, not by the Spaniards, and not from East to West as one might have expected considering the advent of American exploration. An intrepid young champion, in an effort to elude Mexican authorities and regain the fellowship of his comrades, had scaled the "unscaleable wall," effectively breaching the barrier between El Dorado and the United States of America.

Other parties would follow as growing interest in Spanish California developed among an expanding Yankee presence in the West.

In 1833 Captain B.L.E. Bonneville, reportedly on leave from the United States army, dispatched seventy men under the auspices of his premier trail blazer, 35-year-old Joseph Redeford Walker. Setting out to explore the unknown country between Great Salt Lake and the Pacific Ocean, they followed the general course of Humboldt River, until it vanished on the barren landscape beneath the great Sierra escarpment. Zenas Leonard, Bonneville's able clerk, writes, "We continued our course in the direction of *a large mountain which we could see was covered with snow on the summit.*"

The following week was spent searching for a way around or over the great "mountain" barrier. The narrative continues: "The next morning several parties were dispatched in search of a pass over the mountain, and to make search for game; but they all returned in the evening without finding either. The prospect at this time began to grow somewhat gloomy and threatened us with hard times. We were at a complete stand. No one was acquainted with the country, nor no person knew how wide the summit of this mountain was. We had traveled for five days since we arrived at what we supposed to be the summit - were now still surrounded with snow and rugged peaks - the vigour of every man almost exhausted."

In this, their darkest moment, the tiny band of bewildered frontiersmen were approaching a climax; a climax not only in their journey, but in its historic significance. Soon they would behold one of the wonders of the natural world.

"We traveled a few miles every day, still on the top of the mountain, and our course continually obstructed with snow, hills, and rocks." Leonard's journal continues:

"Here we began to encounter in our path, many small streams which would shoot out from under these high snow-banks, and after running a short distance in deep chasms which they have through ages cut in the rocks, precipitate themselves from one lofty precipice to another, until they are exhausted in rain below. Some of these precipices appeared to us to be more than a mile high. Some of the men thought that if we could succeed in descending one of these precipices to the bottom, we might thus work our way into the valley below — but on making several attempts we found it utterly impossible for a man to descend, to say nothing of the horses."

In searching the whole Sierra Nevada one can find but a

JOSEPH REDEFORD WALKER

©1985 THE OAKLAND MUSEUM'S KAHN COLLECTION

YOSEMITE VALLEY, 1876 BY THOMAS HILL

CROSSING THE SIERRA

single location that could have inspired Leonard's description – the Yosemite Valley. Here, then, is the record of its discovery.

What history remembers as the Walker Party had apparently ascended the range along the general course of the old Mono Indian Trail. From the crest they followed very near the present day route of Yosemite National Park's Tioga Road.

Growing ever more desperate and discouraged, the men's spirits were again lifted upon the return of one of their scouts, loaded down with acorns. There was rejoicing in the camp, not only for the value of the food recovered, but for the gratifying evidence that beyond lie a country fair and mild enough to produce acorns. They continued their journey in far better spirits and within three days "arrived at the brink of the mountain."

Here they had a spectacular view as the plains of El Dorado stretched out before them. Now confronted with the problem of how to get down the precipitous incline, they searched out and found another Indian path.

The Walker party was about to make a second historic discovery. "In the last two days traveling," says Leonard, "we have found some trees of the Redwood species, incredibly large – some of which would measure from 16 to 18 fathoms (96 to 108 feet) round the trunk at the height of a man's head from the ground." No one could have invented that description. Published long before anyone else claimed to have seen the "Big Tree" or giant sequoia of the Sierra Nevada, it stands, therefore as the first mention of that sylvan marvel, now known as Sequoiandendron giganteum. It is worthy of note that Leonard observed the similarity between this Sierra giant and the coast redwoods which he later saw in the Santa Cruz Mountains.

Over the barrier and out of the woods at last, Walker's party journeyed unhindered across the great valley of California to the forested slopes of the coast, where they met up with an American ship at Monterey.

This growing Yankee presence in Spanish California was of no little concern to Mexican authorities. Walker's party was greeted with curiosity and suspicion in the colonies of Alta California. No one is really certain just why Bonneville, who accompanied this expedition himself, had organized it in the first place. Enough speculation about the intentions of this and the soon to arrive Fremont party has been generated to fill volumes of novels with espionage and frontier intrigue. At any rate, America's growing interest in a western seaboard erupted shortly thereafter into a full fledged war with Mexico. Such a sequence of events has led some historians to conclude that explorations such as those directed by Captain Bonneville had in reality been conducted under the auspices of United States Government intelligence.

Walker had no intention of repeating his arduous journey over the mountains. Upon the party's return, they searched in vain for a way around the barrier. Finally, unable to locate that which did not exist, they struck out to breach the range once more, this time at the pass that to this day bares his name. North of the Owens Valley he reconnoitered at length with the tracks of his journey west. Happy to find himself on familiar turf, Walker and his men hastened back along the Humboldt, carrying with them more knowledge about Spanish California and its colossal "wall" than that possessed by any other man alive. In the tide of immigration that was about to follow Walker's knowledge would prove invaluable.

Less than a decade following Walker's explorations of California, John C. Fremont, lieutenant in the U.S. Topographical Corp of Engineers, appeared at the base of the grand Sierra. At 30, already a self-assured adventurer, Fremont's orders and motives remain as questionable as those of his predecessor. Yet, quite as determined as the few who had preceded him, he too struck out to cross the seemingly insurmountable range in the dead of winter. Whatever the young man's motives, he did not want for courage or valor. Bringing his party through alive against incredible odds, he not only accomplished a feat of heroic proportions but added tremendously to America's knowledge of Spanish California. With the constitution of a soldier, Fremont nonetheless exhibited an amazing sensitivity towards the natural world. Taking time out in the midst of a blizzard to comment on the spectacular beauty of the Sierra Nevada's peaks and valleys, describing the deep blue color of the Sierra sky, recording his impressions upon discovering Lake Tahoe; for a military man barely surviving in below-freezing temperatures by eating his horse and dog, such recognition of the natural beauty around him must be considered remarkable.

Fremont came to dominate much of America's early activities in California, eventually making his home in the Sierra foothills near present day Mariposa.

The winter of 1846-47 witnessed unprecedented tragedy in the high Sierra. No history of the great range can be told without a moment of solemn reverence being taken to hold back a tear for the ill-fated Donner Party.

Under the leadership of brothers George and Jacob Donner of Illinois, an emigrant train, consisting of twenty covered wagons, headed west for California. Lured by rumors of golden sunshine, perennial harvests, and unlimited opportunities, 87 men, women, and children threw their destinies and belongings together and struck out for the Pacific Coast.

Upon attaining the Continental Divide, serious disputation arose among them over which way to proceed. Against the judgement of George and Jacob the wagon train struck out on an untried route that ended up taking the pioneers through trackless desert and difficult mountain passes. By the time

EASTERN FACE OF THE
SIERRA NEVADA

WESTWARD (following page)
THE COURSE OF EMPIRE
TAKES ITS WAY.
Emanuel Gottlieb Leutze. 1861

A MINER'S BEST FRIEND

the Sierra, their greatest challenge, had been obtained it was already late in the season. Determined to reach the coast, the factioned party, by now at war with one another after having had to abandon supplies, food, and personal treasures, and having suffered much unnecessary discomfort, assaulted the great mountain massif at a pass that would henceforth bare their name. It was late November.

Caught in heavy snow, the weary travelers were forced to "hole up" at what is now Donner Lake. James Reed struck out ahead to cross the range and seek help. Upon attaining Sutter's Fort, near present day Sacramento, a rescue party was immediately dispatched. Men and provisions were unable to get through, however, and the little band of pioneers, trapped below the eastern summit, began to starve to death. Finally, reduced to eating the flesh of their dead, it seems impossible to fathom the horrors that thereafter transpired.

Louis Keseburg, member of the expedition was accused of killing George Donner's wife to steal her money and eat her body. Other scenes of horror, far too graphic for this chronicler to relate, remain among the darkest moments in the history of the Far West.

It was February before help arrived. Three relief parties carried the survivors down the mountain. Many died, even after having been rescued, due to the consequences of exposure and subsequent illness. All told, forty members of the emigrant train perished. The last of the forty-seven survivors was carried off the mountain in April of 1847.

In January of 1848 gold was discovered in the Sierra foothills along the American River. Instigating nothing short of hysteria, news of easy wealth brought the world rushing into El Dorado. Most arrived by ship through San Francisco's Golden Gate. Countless others, dependent upon guides and sketches printed by Walker and Fremont, struck out overland. Few came adequately prepared. Thinking themselves out of danger once past the Rockies, those who chose overland routes struggled across hundreds of miles of desert wasteland only to find themselves staring up at perpendicular granite walls.

A tribute to the spirit that built the American nation, most "girded up their loins" and struck out to conquer the mountain. There are numerous accounts of trials and personal tragedy documenting the experiences of the forty-niners as they struggled to breach this last great barrier before attaining the land of golden dreams.

During the decade that followed, however, the mountains were conquered by sheer numbers. Soon high country passes had been established and roads graded, while through Donner Pass, scene of much human suffering, roared the iron steam engines of the Union Pacific Railroad.

The sequestered position of Yosemite Valley, together with its isolated wilderness location, kept it hidden, even after hordes of gold seekers had overrun the Range of Light. Walker's diary since lost, forty-niners carried on vigorous min-

ing activities thirty miles from the spectacular mountain throne room without any knowledge of its existence.

Just as confrontation with the Indians had lured Spanish soldiers into the Sierra, so it was with the Yanks who senselessly perpetrated crimes against the redman – inciting him to battle.

James D. Savage, a man whose name suggests the very nature of the life he led, arrived early to the gold fields. Having experienced modest success he went into business for himself, opening trading posts at Agua Fria, near Fremont's Mariposa estate, and on the Fresno River, near Coarsegold. His long association with the Indians reflected itself in the frontiersman's domestic situation. Patriarch of five Indian wives, one from each tribal council, Savage thus demonstrated his unique method of diplomacy. Friend to the white man and Indian alike he found himself in a most difficult position when troubles between the two groups escalated.

Indians of the Sierra Nevada had peaceably co-existed for thousands of years. Content with their primitive way of life they managed to remain, for the most part, aloft from Spanish developments along the coast.

YOSEMITE INDIAN

The arrival of Americans in legions, however, led to a completely different situation – resulting in nothing less than total invasion. Bringing with them preconceived notions of the redman, glorious legacies of Indian battles having been handed down by fathers and grandfathers, the Americans needlessly treated the Miwok, Yokut and others with bigotry and disdain. Determined to subjugate or destroy this impediment to their progress, gold seekers overran tribal lands, altered stream courses, churned up the ground, fed the natural food supply of acorn and grain seed to their cattle, hunted off deer and other wild game, and frequently forced themselves upon native Indian women. They thus disrupted irreparably the Indian way of life.

In retaliation, tribal leaders took to raiding miner's camps and settlements. It was a cycle of resistance that had repeated itself over and over again since shortly after the arrival of the Pilgrim Fathers at Plymouth Rock.

In the early spring of 1851, Savage's outpost on the Fresno River was raided by marauding Indians. Two white men were murdered. To prevent reprisals, the Governor of the newly formed State of California called upon Savage to round up the remaining Indian "offenders" and convince them to sign treaties. Such conscription would lead to their removal from the mountains and relocation on reservations established near what is now Fresno. Thus was formed the Mariposa Battalion. Major Savage, at its head, set out to fulfill his commission.

Although most of the Indians agreed to accept the white man's treaties, some of the more resolute refused to leave their mountain strong-holds. Savage had heard of a mysterious valley wherein the hostile Yosemite (Uhumati), or Grizzly Bear tribe, was said to have its villages.

Word reached Teneiya, Chief of the Yosemites (Ahwahnee-chees as they called themselves), that the white man was out to arrest both he and his braves. Rather than allow Savage to find

(continued on page 74)   71

GRIZZLY ADAMS

James Capen Adams was an enterprising New Englander. Leaving behind his cobbler's trade at age 36, he, like so many others, headed west for California in 1849 to seek his fame and fortune. Adams was to find both, albeit in a rather unconventional fashion. From Los Angeles he worked his way to the gold fields, where the determined Yankee made and lost a fortune on three consecutive occasions. Disenchanted, he sought solace in the wilderness of the high Sierra.

Setting up camp near Yosemite Valley, in 1852, Adams began collecting pelts and trapping live animals, for which he found a ready market. It was while thus employed that his fateful meeting with an orphaned grizzly bear cub occurred. James named his newly acquired charge Ben Franklin. He set out to give the youngster a proper upbringing. His life with Ben has since been told and retold to every successive generation of children. James would henceforth and forever remembered adoringly as Grizzly Adams.

Adams, in company with his dog Rambler and his bear Benjamin, traveled the continent. Together they shared many great adventures. Perhaps their most terrific escapade transpired during the spring of 1855 not far from the mountainman's camp in the Sierra high country.

While trapsing through shoulder-high chaparral Adams startled a female grizzly. The huge bruin heaved up on her hind legs and struck James across the head with her front paw, peeling the shaken hunter's scalp down over his eyes. Adams fell head first to the ground whereupon the great bear began to tear through his buckskin at his shoulders and back. James yelled out "St'boy!" to Rambler and Ben, who were not far behind. Ben charged his master's assailant from the front, while Rambler attacked her hindquarters. Thus distracted, the she-bear freed Adams, who quickly grabbed his gun. Laying back his scalp and wiping the blood from his eyes so as to be able to see, he let loose a blood-curdling screetch. The grizzly rose whereupon he shot her through the heart. Ben and Rambler bounded back to camp yelping all the way.

Ben and Adams forever afterwards carried the scars of that conflict. The bond between them thus strengthened, they would remain life-long companions.

THREE BROTHERS

NAMED IN HONOR
OF CHIEF TENIEYA'S
THREE BRAVE SONS

their secret valley home, Teneiya set out to meet with his accuser enroute. That rendezvous took place near present day Wawona. After much discussion and futile debate Teneiya promised to return and lead his people out of the mountains, if allowed to do so on his own reconnaissance. Savage agreed to wait at Wawona for several days, whereupon the Ahwahneechees met their escort and were led down to Fresno. Observing the lack of strong young braves among his reluctant exiles, however, Savage was convinced that Teneiya's warriors were still hiding out in the mysterious "Uhumati" Valley. He therefore insisted on being taken to the village in company with 50 to 60 of his strongest men; their fitness having been ascertained by means of a foot race. Major Savage and Chief Teneiya made their way together through heavy timber to the secret mountain labyrinth. It is fortunate for historians that Lafayette H. Bunnell, among Savage's most "fit" soldiers, was along. The twenty-seven year old recorded events of each day, a journal that would later be considered as priceless to students of Sierra Nevada history.

At Inspiration Point the intrepid battalion came into full view of what has since been heralded as the most incredible valley in the world. So overcome were they by such beauty that Bunnell recorded, "I found my eyes in tears with emotion." He describes the spectacle just as it greets adventurers today:

"The grandeur of the scene was softened by the haze that hung over the valley – light as gossamer – and by the clouds which partially dimmed the higher cliffs and mountains. This obscurity of vision but increased the awe with which I beheld it, and as I looked, a peculiar, exalted sensation seemed to fill my whole being."

Savage's assumption had been correct. Upon marching into the spectacular mountain chamber soldiers spied Indian braves running for cover. Yosemite Valley's "discovery" was marred by tragedy when the Ahwahneechee lads refused to surrender. Teneiya witnessed the murder of his son and removal of his courageous braves by force from their beautiful Valley of Ahwahnee (Tall Grass), breaking both the old man's heart and spirit.

The mysterious Valley of Uhumati, as Savage had called it, became known to the modern world as Yosemite (anglicized version of Uhumati), its mysterious beauty a source of wonder and intrigue that would attract millions.

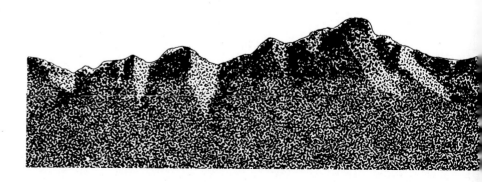

**T**rend setters from the beginning, Californians immediately recognized the singularity of the Yosemite. Early tourists had included publishing tycoon Horace Greeley who heralded the valley as "The greatest marvel on the continent." Community-conscious citizens set out to preserve the pristine nature of Yosemite, together with its unique giant sequoias, before either could be exploited.

In 1860 a popular young preacher from Boston by the name of Thomas Starr King arrived in San Francisco. Having accepted a call from the Unitarian Church to aid its new and struggling California congregation, Starr King, as his associates called him, perceived in his calling an opportunity to familiarize himself with the mountains of the West. A lover of nature, he had just published a work entitled "The White Mountains." His study, serialized in New England Papers, generated much interest in both Starr King as a writer, and the New Hampshire wilderness that he had chosen as his first source of material.

Of particular interest to the young evangelist were the splendid marvels to be seen in the "Yo Semite" Valley. During his first summer in California he took leave of the pulpit long enough to explore the famed Sierra landmark. So overwhelmed was he by what he saw that he determined to share such boundless beauty with the following he had gathered through his earlier writings. A series of articles were run in various New England dailies, bringing further acclaim to both their author and to the Yosemite. Describing trees "in whose trunk Bunker Hill Monument could have been inserted and hidden," and waterfalls "the height of six Park Street Spires," the success of Starr King's journalistic endeavors encouraged him to use such influence toward preserving the beauty he had imparted so vividly to the American public.

Sharing his dream for the protection of the Yosemite were more pressing issues, however. An eloquent speaker and passionate opponent of slavery, he fought tirelessly to preserve California as a free state for the Union.

Sudden illness, brought on by over-exertion, claimed the life of the beloved pastor, just months before fulfillment of his campaign to save the natural splendor of Yosemite. On June 30, 1864 President Abraham Lincoln took time out from Civil War concerns to sign into law a bill that granted Yosemite Valley and the Mariposa Grove of Big Trees (giant sequoias) to the State of California, to be "preserved for all time." It was the first such act in history, setting a precedent for the soon-to-follow National Park Service.

GLACIER POINT

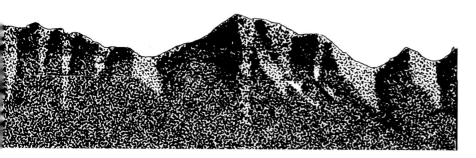

FREDERICK LAW OLMSTEAD

FATHER OF LANDSCAPE
ARCHITECTURE

ollowing a dispute with officials in New York City over his assigned task to design Central Park, Frederick Law Olmstead came West to manage the Mariposa estate of General John C. Fremont. Thus introduced to the Sierra Nevada, America's foremost pioneer of "landscape architecture" found himself uniquely qualified to direct the affairs of the newly formed Yosemite Forest Reservation. His skills hardly unnoticed, he was promptly called upon to serve as the Park's first Commissioner.

His was a fateful appointment for the destiny of Yosemite Valley. No finer man could there have been to guide the fledgling preserve through its first critical decade.

Of the glorious natural heirloom entrusted to his qualified care he wrote, "Union of the deepest sublimity with the deepest beauty of nature, not in one feature or another, not in one part or one scene or another, not in any landscape that can be framed by itself, but all around and wherever the visitor goes, constitutes the Yo Semite, the greatest glory of nature."

The great virtue of natural scenery, he concluded, was in the fact that "the enjoyment of scenery employs the mind without fatigue and yet exercises it; tranquilizes it and yet enlivens it; and thus, through the influence of the mind over the body, gives the effect of refreshing rest and reinvigoration to the whole system."

And so it was that in a few short years that which had been viewed as a great obstacle to be overcome and subdued had suddenly become perceived as a source of both mental and physical health; a balm to soothe the soul of man.

mong the early visitors to arrive at Yosemite was a young man by the name of John Muir. Scottish born and midwestern bred, Muir possessed a keen sensitivity to nature. In search of "the order that governs all things in the Universe" he had come West. Upon his arrival in San Francisco, legend has it that the young traveler inquired as to where the wild country could be found. His informant pointed towards the Sierra, and Muir was on his way.

The Scot's arrival in Yosemite Valley during the spring of 1868 was fortuitous not only for him but for the Sierra Nevada as well. It is said that Muir shouted for joy upon first seeing the Yosemite. His exuberance for this "most holy mansion of the mountains" never ceased. After having wandered the West his destiny had finally caught up with him. Here he found the answer to his quest. Everything about him seemed to testify to orderly processes that exemplified eternal principles. "God himself seems to be always doing his best here," he wrote. For the next few years Muir accepted any kind of employment that would allow him access to live in and study the Sierra Nevada. Farmhand, millworker, shepherd, and hotel-clerk – through it all he kept his journals, recording his first hand observations and personal impressions.

"The Mighty Sierra," wrote Muir, "is so gloriously colored, so radiant, it seemed not clothed with light but wholly com-

posed of it, like the wall of some celestial city. Then it seemed to me the Sierra should be called not the Nevada or Snowy Range, but the Range of Light. And after ten years spent in the heart of it, rejoicing and wandering, bathing in the glorious floods of light, seeing the sunbursts of morning among the icy peaks, the noonday radiance on the trees and rocks and snow, the flush of the alpenglow, and a thousand dashing waterfalls with their marvelous abundance of irised spray, it still seems to me above all others the Range of Light, the most divinely beautiful of all the mountain chains I have ever seen."

Granite monoliths and leaping cataracts had made an indelible impression upon the youngman. "As long as I live," Muir recorded, "I will everafter hear waterfalls and birds and winds sing. I'll acquaint myself with the glaciers and wild gardens, and get as near to the heart of the world as I can."

Beyond the splendid Yosemite Valley, Muir became intrigued with the high country and above all by the stupendous groves of giant sequoias that graced the Sierra's conifer belt. A spiritual and sensitive man, he witnessed with concern the invasion of cattlemen and shepherds into this primeval realm of virgin wilderness. He saw railroads and speculators picking up land and water rights. His heart reached out to the earth and to her "thousands needing rest — the weary in soul and limb, toilers in town and plain, dying for what these grand old woods can give."

Determined to familiarize himself better with the situation, to properly assess the extent of the territory thus threatened, he set out in company with his mule, Brownie, to wander nearly the entire length of the Sierra Nevada. He shouted with exhilaration each time he discovered another grove of "Big Trees" (giant sequoia) on the horizon. Often he would sit quietly with his cup of tea in hand straining to hear the sound of a sawmill in the distance. He wondered if these magnificent Sierra redwoods, which had taken thousands of years to mature, would survive to see the twentieth century.

Upon Muir's return to Yosemite Valley, formulation of a plan to protect and preserve all that he had seen had begun to take shape in his mind. Using the giant sequoia as a catalyst for his proposals, he determined to first make the beauty and value of wilderness better understood by the masses. Once accomplished, he was certain that they would rally to his support and thus aid in the preservation of the Sierra Nevada's natural state. And so it happened. From that moment until his death in 1914 John Muir worked incessantly for the preservation of the natural world; writing, lecturing, inspiring, persuading. His following grew. Beginning with a determination to save the giant sequoia, "King of all the conifers of the world, noblest of a noble race," he wrote, "any fool can destroy trees. They cannot run away, and if they could they would still be destroyed, chased and hunted down as long as fun and dollar could be got out of their bark hides, branching horns, or magnificent bole backbones. God had cared for these trees, saved them from drought, disease, avalanches, and a thousand floods; but he cannot save them from fools – only Uncle Sam can do that."

JOHN MUIR

AMERICA'S MOST
BELOVED CONSERVATIONIST

MUIR AND ROOSEVELT
AT GLACIER POINT

THE SIERRA CLUB WAS
ORGANIZED IN 1892 UNDER
THE LEADERSHIP OF JOHN
MUIR, "TO EXPLORE, ENJOY,
AND RENDER ACCESSIBLE
THE MOUNTAIN REGIONS OF
THE PACIFIC COAST; TO
PUBLISH AUTHENTIC INFOR-
MATION CONCERNING THEM;
TO ENLIST THE SUPPORT
AND COOPERATION OF THE
PEOPLE AND THE GOVERN-
MENT IN PRESERVING THE
FORESTS AND OTHER
NATURAL FEATURES OF THE
SIERRA NEVADA."

And so began John Muir's campaign on the United States Government to save the giant sequoias while there was still time.

Perhaps the highlight in this chapter of Sierra Nevada history came during four days in mid-May of 1903.

In a communique to one of his close associates Muir wrote modestly "an influential man from Washington wants to make a trip into the Sierra with me, and I might be able to do some forest good in freely talking around the campfire."

The man Muir spoke of was President Theodore Roosevelt. Their sudsequent "chats" around the campfire resulted in the setting aside of over a million acres of irreplaceable scenic grandeur in national parks and forests scattered across the Sierra Nevada.

At the conclusion of his "camping trip" the President assured his host that the experience had been "bully." Calling Yosemite "the most beautiful place in the world," Mr. Roosevelt went on to tell both John Muir and the press that he had enjoyed the time of his life. "Just think of where I was last night," the President exulted, "Up there (Glacier Point) amid the pines and silver firs, in the Sierran solitude, and without a tent I passed one of the most pleasant nights of my life."

Soon virtually all logging of the giant sequoia had stopped. The boundaries of the Yosemite Preserve had been expanded and taken over by the Federal Government as a National Park, following after the example of the Yellowstone. Two other such "Parks" had been created at Sequoia and General Grant (later enlarged and incorporated as part of Kings Canyon National Park).

Realizing what could be achieved, Muir organized his flock into a group that has since become the world's most powerful advocate of conservation – the Sierra Club.

ontroversy and conflict continue to challenge the realm of the great stone mountains. Imperious and grand they nevertheless cannot withstand, unguarded, the growing impact of the ever-increasing millions who seek out their sanctuary each year.

Today world class ski resorts and casinos adorn the shores of Lake Tahoe, while elsewhere, in isolated terrain that challenged the likes of Jedediah Smith and Joseph Redeford Walker *thousands* follow in their since proven footsteps, trekking the high country trails. Visitation to Yosemite Valley approaches 3 million guests annually. Simply stated, seeking sanctuary in the high country threatens the sanctuary sought. For ever increasing millions "going to the woods" is still "going home," To preserve this legacy is one of modern man's greatest challenges.

Yosemite and the high Sierra today continue to afford endless scenic beauty and spaciousness for the over-civilized man and woman. However long you stay, the experience will enrich your life. Indelible impressions are made upon the soul that will last a lifetime. Let the peace and grandeur of the high country fill your soul. Savor it. Carry it with you back to the urban domain of ivory towers. Release it there to fill your own world with the finery, splendor, and inner solitude of Nature's order.

Northern Sierra

TAHOE ● RENO

ALAN CAREY

WILLIAM NEILL

ED COOPER

Gem of the Sierra, Lake Tahoe, with its crystal blue waters and pine-clad shores, forms a picture postcard setting for distinctive mountain homes and world class resorts.

Formed at the end of the last great Ice Age by melting glaciers, Tahoe's 12 mile wide expanse sits like a giant bowl amidst rugged peaks, many towering in excess of 10,000 feet above the Nevada desert.

Scenic Highway 395 skirts the eastern flank of the mighty Sierra, affording spectacular vistas of mountain citadels, pine and aspen forests, and desert wilderness.

EASTERN SIERRA

BRIDGEPORT • MAMMOTH • BISHOP

ROY MURPHY

Bridgeport (below), with its Victorian Courthouse, circa 1880, and tourist trade, serves as gateway to some of the finest fishing and hunting grounds in the state.

Silent Mono Lake (right), an inland sea dotted with islands of volcanic origin, is so alkaline that only tiny brine shrimp inhabit its waters.

Southernmost peak of the Sierra, stately Mount Whitney (below right), near Bishop, at 14,495 feet is the highest summit in the continental United States.

ED COOPER

ED COOPER

Central Sierra

YOSEMITE

Shrine of the Sierra, Yosemite Valley with its towering peaks, lacy waterfalls, and park-like meadows is among the world's most beautiful garden spots. Here powerful Yosemite Falls (right) plummets over the rim of the valley in a drop of 2,425 feet, making it the second highest waterfall in the world. Across the chasm, beautiful Bridalveil Falls (below right) pours into the mountain throneroom from high country snowfields beyond.

Vernal Falls' mist trail (below) is a popular hiking destination for many Yosemite visitors.

PAT O'HARA

ED COOPER

ED COOPER

ED COOPER

EMIL FORLER

splash of color to the many world famous monoliths of Yosemite National Park. The Sentinal (left) guardian of the Valley, El Capitan (below) and Half Dome (below left) are among the most prominent features of this glaciated labyrinth.

ED COOPER

EMIL FORLER

In winter the glory of Yosemite is shrouded beneath a mantle of white. El Capitan (above), assumes a cold, steel blue appearance. The Grand Old Ahwahnee Hotel (far right) beckons chilled mountaineers to step inside and warm themselves by the hearth of her great stone fireplace.

Further south, in Sequoia National Park, magnificent General Sherman, at 275 feet in height and 37 feet in diameter, stands like a king, reportedly the largest living thing on earth, cloaked in a winter garb of snow.

Winter sport enthusiasts take to the mountains en mass to indulge in cross country ski expeditions and downhill slalom competitions at any one of a number of outstanding Sierra resorts.

EMIL FORLER

ROY MURPHY

EMIL FORLER

EMIL FORLER

DAVE GRABER

PAT O'HARA

ED COOPER

EMIL FORLER

Spring comes late to the high Sierra. Green grass and tiny alpine blossoms blanket Tuolumne Meadows (far left), snow-fed rivers and falls swell to overflowing (above left), great bears (above far left) awake from their winter slumber (California bears apparently find California sunshine as intoxicating as do we humans. Not true hibernators, they are often seen ambling about the snowdrifts, foraging and playing in the warm sunshine). Unique features such as the Devil's Postpile (left) are popular high country destinations for outdoor enthusiast.

ED COOPER

SOUTHERN SIERRA

SEQUOIA • KINGS CANYON

Spectacular Kings Canyon (above) constitutes the Sierra's most profound gash. Snow-fed cascades, such as Grizzly Falls (above right), add to the splendor of this alpine wilderness. The four guardsmen (far right) greet visitors near the entrance to the giant sequoia's domain in Sequoia National Park. Here, among these forest titans, the little chickaree (above far right), or Douglas squirrel, makes his home.

JAMES BLANK

ALAN CAREY

ED COOPER

ED COOPER

The giant sequoia stands in an environment whose scenic grandeur underscores that of the trees own majesty. Almost as massive as the alps of France, Switzerland, and Italy combined, California's Sierra Nevada forms the highest unbroken chain of mountains in the continental United States. Sporting a crest that surmounts 14,000 feet, with canyons that plummet to depths of as much as 8,000 feet, this formidable range intimidated early pioneers and frontiersmen; successfully isolating the colonies of New Spain from an expanding Yankee nation for nearly one hundred years.

Along the less precipitous western slope of this imposing stone battlement stretches California's second great forest primeval. Like the coastal "rain forest," it too is dominated by redwood giants. Towering over this timberzone of impressive tree growth stand the regal sequoia giants, distant cousins to the coast redwood. Prehistoric groves and forests of these largest of all living things lend an aura of other-worldliness to their behemoth mountain setting.

When Sequoia and General Grant National Parks (the latter was later absorbed into the much larger Kings Canyon Park) were first formed, back in 1890, they effectively brought under protection the very heart of the Sierra redwood empire during an age when the monarch dendroids were threatened by logging interests. Today, thanks to the efforts of men like John Muir (father of American conservation), the giant sequoia maintains its reign over the high country.

As two national parks, joined end to end, Sequoia - Kings Canyon encompass a superlative stretch of American wilderness. Granite peaks, gorges, nearly a thousand rock-bound glacial lakes, flowering alpine meadows, virgin forest, and of course the mighty Sequoiandendron giganteum (giant sequoia) are all safeguarded in their pristine condition as twentieth century man's legacy to future generations.

Such splendor culminates along the eastern boundary of the parks, where lofty Mount Whitney, capstone of the great Sierra massif, towers at 14,495 feet - the highest point in the continental United States. Seemingly a god made of stone, the giant mountain stands silent watch over a great American treasure.

ED COOPER

EPILOGUE

Symbol of all things wild and free, the Sierra Bighorn, like wilderness itself, is today both rare and endangered.

Less than a century ago America's frontier wilderness was viewed as something hostile; an enemy to be subdued and overcome, an obstacle in the path of progress. By very definition the word "wilderness" signifies a wasted or barren region.

Today, in America, that notion has changed. Both wilderness and the population of wildlife that it sustains have come to be perceived as a precious commodity of which very little remains. To further exploit this rapidly diminishing "resource" is a question that persists as one of this nation's most controversial issues. The choice to preserve, in a pristine state, the wild character of these isolated regions has consequently become the obsession of many enlightened citizens.

No longer viewed as something threatening, the wilderness is interpreted by contemporary man as being the ultimate expression of the Master's plan; that all living things be born wild and free. "It is here," wrote western novelist Zane Grey, "I feel the *happiness* that dwells in wilderness alone."

The mighty Sierra Nevada affords one of America's last great strongholds of wilderness. To bequeath such a treasure to our children seems both wise and prudent; for to do so would help to preserve the very spirit that *is* America. Here, in these untamed mountains, awaits adventures in independence; experiences that nurture within the breast that indomitable desire to remain wild and free, to resist oppression, and to respect the rights of all living things to share in such freedom.

To preserve wilderness is to preserve the spirit of the land that dwells within each of us, the spirit that makes us uniquely "American."

BIBLIOGRAPHY

Arno, Stephen F., "Discovering Sierra Trees," Yosemite, California, Yosemite National History Association, 1973.

Bennett, Ross, "Yosemite," National Geographics - The New America's Wonderlands - Our National Parks, Washington, D.C., National Geographic Society, 1980.

Brooks, Paul, "Ansel Adams - Yosemite and The Range of Light." Boston, New York Graphic Society, 1979.

Collings, Adam Randolph, "California - The Golden State." Anaheim, California, Adam Randolph Collings, Inc., 1982.

Ditton, Richard P., and Donald E. McHenry, "Yosemite Road Guide." Yosemite, California, Yosemite Natural History Association, 1976.

Editors, "The Magnificent Continent." Chicago, Rand McNally, 1975.

Farquhar, Francis P., "History of the Sierra Nevada." Berkeley, University of California Press, 1965.

Godfrey, Elizabeth, "Yosemite Indians." Yosemite, California, Yosemite Natural History Association, 1978 Rev. Ed.

Heizer, Robert F., and Albert B. Elsasser, "The Natural World of the California Indians." Berkeley, University of California Press, 1980.

Hill, Mary, "Geology of the Sierra Nevada." Berkeley, University of California Press, 1975.

Hubbard, Douglass H., "Yosemite - A Golden Regional Guide." New York, Golden Press, 1970.

Huning, James R., "Hot, Dry, Cold, Wet, and Windy - A Weather Primer for the National Parks of the Sierra Nevada." Yosemite, California, Yosemite Natural History Association, 1978.

Jensen, Peter, "Yosemite - Shrine of the Sierra." Anaheim, California, Randy Collings Productions, 1982.

Kauffman, John M., "Sequoia - Kings Canyon." National Geographics - The New America's Wonderlands - Our National Parks, Washington, D.C., National Geographic Society, 1980.

Matthes, Francois E., "The Incomparable Valley - A Geologic Interpretation of the Yosemite." Berkeley, University of California Press, 1950.

Miller, Cranes, and Richard S. Hyslop, "California - The Geography of Diversity." Pomona, Mayfield Publishing Company, 1983.

Morgenson, Dana, "The Four Seasons of Yosemite." Yosemite, California, Yosemite Park and Curry Company, 1978.

Muir, John, "The Coniferous Forests and Big Trees of the Sierra Nevada." Golden, Colorado, Outbooks, 1980.

Muir, John, "The Mountains of California." Berkeley, California, Tenspeed Press, 1977.

Muir, John, "The Yosemite." Garden City, New York, Doubleday and Company, Inc., 1962.

Perry, John, and Jane Greverus Perry, "The Sierra Club Guide to the Natural Areas of California." San Francisco, Sierra Club Books, 1983.

Sargent, Shirley, "John Muir in Yosemite." Yosemite, Flying Spur Press, 1971.

Storer, Tracy I. and Lloyd P. Tevis, Jr., "California Grizzly." Lincoln, University of Nebraska Press, 1978.

Storer, Tracy I. and Robert L. Usinger, "Sierra Nevada Natural History." Berkeley, University of California Press, 1963.

Trexler, Keith A., "The Tioga Road." Yosemite, California, Yosemite Natural History Association, 1980.

Whitney, Stephen, "A Sierra Club Naturalist's Guide - The Sierra Nevada." San Francisco, Sierra Club Books, 1979.

INDEX

ACKNOWLEDGEMENTS

No project as involved as the production and publication of a new book is ever completed without the contributions of time and talent from many dedicated individuals. YOSEMITE AND THE HIGH SIERRA is no exception.

The creator of this book wishes to express his appreciaton first and foremost to his mother and father for their love, encouragement, and assistance, generously imparted throughout the years; to Henry Berrey (director emeritus of the Yosemite Natural History Association), Herbie Sansum (park interpretor at Yosemite National Park), and John Palmer (chief park naturalist at Sequoia-Kings Canyon National Parks), for their generous assistance and scholarly advice.

The publisher wishes to acknowledge the guidance and support of Luke Hesse, Bob Carter, and Bruce Chambers (all of Jefferies Lithograph) for their confidence and support, photographers and artists who have remained supportive throughout the years and to Divine providence for providing the subject matter for this book (namely Yosemite itself) as well as for the inspiration and the means with which to produce it.

ADAM RANDOLPH COLLINGS
incorporated

THE END

THE·AMERICAN·EXPERIENCE